Living
Without Fear

JEREMY P. TARCHER/PENGUIN

a member of Penguin Group (USA) Inc.

New York

Living
Without Fear

ERNEST HOLMES

Compiled and Edited by
WILLIS H. KINNEAR

JEREMY P. TARCHER/PENGUIN
Published by the Penguin Group
Penguin Group (USA) Inc., 375 Hudson Street, New York, New York 10014, USA ·
Penguin Group (Canada), 90 Eglinton Avenue East, Suite 700, Toronto, Ontario M4P 2Y3,
Canada (a division of Pearson Penguin Canada Inc.) · Penguin Books Ltd, 80 Strand,
London WC2R 0RL, England · Penguin Ireland, 25 St Stephen's Green, Dublin 2, Ireland
(a division of Penguin Books Ltd) · Penguin Group (Australia), 250 Camberwell Road,
Camberwell, Victoria 3124, Australia (a division of Pearson Australia Group Pty Ltd) ·
Penguin Books India Pvt Ltd, 11 Community Centre, Panchsheel Park, New Delhi–110 017,
India · Penguin Group (NZ), 67 Apollo Drive, Rosedale, North Shore 0632, New Zealand
(a division of Pearson New Zealand Ltd) · Penguin Books (South Africa) (Pty) Ltd,
24 Sturdee Avenue, Rosebank, Johannesburg 2196, South Africa

Penguin Books Ltd, Registered Offices: 80 Strand, London WC2R 0RL, England

First Jeremy P. Tarcher/Penguin edition 2010
Copyright © 1962 by *Science of Mind* Publications

Published simultaneously in Canada

Most Tarcher/Penguin books are available at special quantity discounts for bulk purchase for sales
promotions, premiums, fund-raising, and educational needs. Special books or book excerpts also can be
created to fit specific needs. For details, write Penguin Group (USA) Inc. Special Markets, 375 Hudson
Street, New York, NY 10014.

Library of Congress Cataloging-in-Publication Data

Holmes, Ernest, 1887–1960.
Living without fear / Ernest Holmes.
p. cm.
Collected from the earlier issues of Science of mind magazine.
ISBN 978-1-58542-813-7
1. Thought and thinking.   2. Self-actualization (Psychology).   3. Fear.
I. Science of mind.   II. Title.
BF441.H55   2010   2010016015
299'.93—dc22

Printed in the United States of America
1   3   5   7   9   10   8   6   4   2

BOOK DESIGN BY NICOLE LAROCHE

Contents

PART ONE
Freedom from Fear Is Possible

Foreword

This is the second in the series of Annual Editions of *Science of Mind* magazine to bring together the miscellaneous writings of Ernest Holmes.

The material in this Edition is taken from the earliest issues of *Science of Mind* magazine. Many of these articles were based on Dr. Holmes's lectures during what was probably his most dynamic period as a teacher of modern metaphysics.

A great deal of the material in the early issues of the magazine was incorporated in the revised edition of the textbook, *The Science of Mind*. However, equally valuable material was of necessity omitted due to limitations of space. Some of it has been brought together to make this book.

From one point of view this might be said to be a supplement to his textbook.

For over thirty years this material has been unavailable to the reading public, and it is hoped that now that it has been brought to light it will offer new hope, inspiration, and instruction to many new and old readers. Here we find Ernest Holmes presented to us in the same manner that first established him as one of the great religious philosophers and spiritual leaders of our day.

WILLIS KINNEAR

Introduction

We spend most of our lives trying to avoid what we do not like and seeking to experience more of those things that bring us pleasure, happiness, and well-being. However, in doing this we find ourselves in an almost continual state of fear in one or more of its many forms. We fear what we do not like, and also fear we will not have what we do like.

Worry, crisis, and anxiety seem to plague most people, often to the extent that life is something to be suffered through rather than to be lived with joy. This does not mean that we shall ever be free of all problems, but rather that life and living present a continual challenge, which we should learn to master instead of allowing it to master us.

No one imposes fear upon us, rather we create it for ourselves in our own thoughts and emotions. What we need to realize is that we have just as much freedom to eliminate fear as we have in creating it.

That there is an obvious need to secure our freedom from our self-created and self-imposed fears is found in those sciences which deal with the mind and the body. Any evidence of fear in our thought, whether it be large or small, can have subtle and far-reaching consequences. Unless properly handled the entire process of thought can become unbalanced and misdirected. Similarly, fear seems to be able to affect the function and structure of almost every part of the body.

Two questions immediately arise: To what extent can we afford to let ourselves become subject to the destructive thoughts of fear which we have established for ourselves? What can we do to free ourselves from them and replace them with other thoughts and ideas which will contribute to our welfare?

The escape from fear does not involve a retreat from living, but it does mean that our reactions to experiences should not be allowed to overwhelm us but should lead to constructive action. This implies that there should be a renewing of the mind so that its reactions to life are not negative, and that a watch should be maintained on our processes of thought so that they are maintained on a positive, constructive, creative level.

If a person seeks to free himself from limitations which

his fears have imposed upon him, it will also be necessary for him to free himself from those ideas which have nourished and kept the fears alive to wreak their damage.

The purpose of the material in this book is to show you the pathway that may enable you to start your journey to a new freedom, a freedom from fear, and a greater participation in all those things which make life more worthwhile.

You can find a freedom from fear, and you can discover the ways and means to achieve more of what your heart desires. The journey can be made, the goals can be achieved. But it is something that no one else can do for you, for the attainment rests in the processes of your own thought.

The challenge in life and living is to what degree we can learn to think constructively. This book can show you the way, but the actual traveling of that way is up to you. And in your journey from fear to freedom you will be making the greatest discovery any man can make—the discovery of yourself!

W. K.

*Living
Without Fear*

Freedom from Fear Is Possible

From time immemorial it has been almost instinctive for man, when confronted with fear, to turn to what he has considered a Power greater than himself; to seek release or protection from situations and conditions which have threatened what he considered a normal, natural existence.

This turning to a greater Power has been common to all men, at all times, and is an inherent aspect of all religious beliefs.

Primarily it is an act of thought, but it is also accompanied by action commensurate with the nature of the thought. This act of thought has been called many things, but is commonly identified as prayer. However, much that has passed as prayer has been ineffective in establishing the freedom sought.

What we seek to determine is the nature of man and the prayer which produces desired results.

Get Rid of Superstitions

Science is defined as "knowledge of facts, laws, and proximate causes, gained and verified by exact observation and correct thinking."

Superstition is defined as "a belief founded on irrational feelings" and as "a belief in a religious system regarded (by others than the believer) as unreasonable."

Supernatural is defined as "that which is outside the range of the accepted course of nature; that which transcends nature and includes the Creator."

Nature is defined as "the system of natural existences, forces, changes, and events, regarded as distinguished from, or exclusive of, the supernatural."

From the above stated definitions we gather that science

is that which we know something about or have a definite knowledge of. Superstition is an unreasonable belief, especially in regard to religious convictions and our ideas of God. The supernatural is that which we do not understand or have any definite knowledge of, but might be that which includes the Creator, while nature means natural existence.

It appears from these definitions that the dictionary defines the supernatural from a superstitious standpoint, for it clearly states that the supernatural is outside the range of nature but includes the being of God. The definition is not scientific but superficial.

We are living in a scientific age, therefore in an age of a more or less exact knowledge of many things. But can we say that we have exact knowledge of ultimate causes other than that gathered from their effects? *We do not see the cause of anything.* All that we do see is the effect of invisible causes.

We are daily confronted by a creation the cause of which no man sees. This cause is what we mean by the supernatural or that which transcends nature. And man has given to this cause the name of God or Spirit.

Of course we have the right to assume a cause when we see an effect, for there can be no effect without some cause from which it rises. If superstition is that which is outside the range of our accepted ideas of nature, but that which might include the Creator, then it follows that most of our ideas about the Creator must be superstitions.

Now is it, or is it not, superstitious to believe in God or Spirit? Can the scientist call the religionist superstitious? or can the religionist call the scientist superstitious? The religionist believes in a God higher and more powerful than the natural world as we now understand it. The scientist believes in a power which transcends the material world but is part of ultimate Reality.

Suppose we combine the beliefs of the scientist and the religionist and see what we will have. We will have God, the Intelligence above nature (which the scientist says we do not understand), and we will have nature and natural causes which we understand only in part.

It would seem as though there were room for both the scientist and the religionist. The religionist believes in God, the scientist also believes in God, and there need be no conflict between the two. But both the religionist and the scientist may easily become *superstitious*. The religionist is superstitious when he believes that God works outside of nature or contrary to it, and the scientist is superstitious when he believes that there is any natural existence which is exclusive of the supernatural.

Science of Mind teaches that the supernatural world is

the spiritual world and at the same time the spiritual world permeates the natural world. One is the cause, the other the effect. Both are true and each is necessary if there is to be any creation.

Creation is a fact, therefore the Creator also must be a fact. By the Creator we mean the intelligent Principle running through everything.

How do we know that there is such an intelligent Principle? The answer is simple but conclusive: because we are intelligent enough to recognize Intelligence!

The dictionary defines God as "the one Supreme Being, self-existent and eternal; the infinite maker, sustainer, and ruler of the universe." It is an axiom of pure reason that there must be and is such an infinite power in the universe. God is an undivided whole, therefore omnipresent. God, then, is not only above but is also in His creation. The natural is permeated with the supernatural; it causes, flows through, and gives rise to conditions. God is not only *above* what He does; He is also *in* what He does.

The scientist, observing the natural world, is watching God at work. And as God always works through Law (for this is His nature), the scientist is studying a world of law which he is more or less able to understand.

Let us consider evolution and growth as the series of

steps by which a single cell develops or grows into a multi-cellular organism, either in the development of all life or in a single life. We do not see that which does the evolving, but its result—the thing evolved.

Law is the rule by which certain actions take place; everything in the universe is governed by exact laws, otherwise the universe would be a chaos. We do not see any law, we see what it does and how it acts. *Law is a part of the invisible government of the universe.*

In dealing with facts and actions of every kind we are dealing with law, and insofar as we understand the law governing any fact or action, we understand the action. But we understand the actor only through the act. Causes are partly revealed and partly concealed. Any given cause is ascertained by a careful observation of its effects. In proving effects we establish causes in understanding effects we penetrate the nature of causes.

It is certain that there can be no effect without a cause; it is just as certain that there can be no cause without some effect. Science deals with effects and in this way penetrates into causes. In the effect, it is dealing with the natural world; in its idea of the cause, it is dealing with the supernatural or spiritual world.

Science of Mind takes into account both the cause and

the effect. It affirms both, each in its place. It does not deny the one and affirm the other, but it does affirm that the one is the cause of the other.

We are living in a universe of spontaneous Intelligence and of absolute Law. Of this we are certain, since we, ourselves, have spontaneous intelligence but are, at the same time, subject to exact laws.

But the question might be raised: How can spontaneous intelligence be subject to exact laws? The answer is that it is the *nature of being* to be this way. The answer is both sensible and adequate. Law is necessary to the universe. It could not be run without law, but the very fact that we can cognize law proves a spontaneous element in creation.

To believe in a God who transcends law is superstitious; to believe in a law which is outside the nature of intelligence is a mistake. To accept both is the truth. To accept an infinite Intelligence in the universe is the only way to account for our own lives; to understand the Law of Life is to enter into the nature of this Intelligence. *We must accept God as both Life and Law.*

God is self-existent as Life and as Law. God did not make God, hence God did not make Law. God did not make God, hence God did not make Life. God, Life, and Law are One, coexistent and coeternal. God as Life expresses Himself through Law. This Law, being an invariable part of the universe, can be relied upon.

It would be superstitious to suppose that by prayer we cause God to change His laws or the way they work. God is Law and cannot contradict His own nature. But, if God is Intelligence as well as Law, it would be a mistake to suppose that this Intelligence cannot respond to our intelligence. This response would not be supernatural but Divinely natural.

When the scientist calls upon the Intelligence within him to direct his thought, he is calling upon God, for the Spirit is everywhere present in Its entirety. The scientist who is truly religious will always surpass the one who discounts the possibility of thinking God's thought after Him.

To suppose that God helps some and not others is superstitious. To suppose that God is ready to help all is both scientific and sensible. It is the nature of God to express Himself. This we know because it is true of our own natures. Whenever our minds are receptive to the Divine influx there is a flowing of God through us, according to exact Law. To deny this Divine inflow is to deny our own natures and shut the door to our own possibilities.

When the scientist thinks, he affirms Intelligence; when he discovers how things work, he affirms Law. Intelligence is spontaneous, Law is automatic. God works through Law, therefore all Law is of the nature of Truth and Reality, whether it be the law of evolution, of chemical reactions, or of gravitation; or whether it be the most subtle law we know of, the "law of mental action and reaction."

There is no law known but that we can affirm it to be a part of the Divine nature. We do not deny Law but that which contradicts Law. We affirm Intelligence and Law as necessary to creation, and we affirm creation as the result of Intelligence and Law.

Abundance cannot produce limitation nor can freedom give birth to bondage. Perfection cannot create imperfection, nor completion create incompletion. That which to us appears incomplete and imperfect is the result of an incomplete and an imperfect understanding of Reality. We are but children in the process of an eternal evolution.

If God is already perfect, free, deathless, and complete, it would be impossible for this Perfection to cognize anything less than Itself. We do not change the nature of Reality through prayer, and it would be superstitious to suppose that we do or can. But, through prayer and meditation we enter into the nature of Reality and partake of this nature. Not that God changes, but that we change our attitude toward God.

The scientist does not pray that the principle of his science may be true, but that he may enter into an understanding of a principle which is already true. As he enters in, he partakes. The religionist should not pray for God to be God, but that he may enter into the Divine nature. The nature of Reality is immutable Law and Order and it cannot be changed by prayer, but when we stand in the shadow of the Almighty we shall no longer be blown by the winds of chance. There is a warm responsiveness from the Spirit to all who contact It in the right way. But this is always Its way. Not our way, but the way of Truth.

We cannot pray to the Principle of Perfection to feed and clothe us and in so doing alter Its exact Law of Cause and Effect. What we can do is to avail ourselves of the Law of Abundance, then we shall experience plenty while the nature of God remains unchanged. There is no special creation. All is Law and all is Order and everything is Divine when rightly understood.

Who and What You Are

M an is a triad—a threefold unity. He is physical, having an objective body; mental, having a conscious, emotional, and subjective reaction to his environment; and spiritual, having a self-knowing mind.

The full nature of man constitutes the law of his being. He is a little world within a big world, but he is largely ignorant of his true nature and this ignorance brings upon him the very bondage, limitation, and fear from which he suffers.

If we were able to remove the entire realm of consciousness from man there would be nothing left, or if anything *should be* left we could not know it. We realize then that the entire being of man, insofar as we can understand his being, must consist of different states of consciousness. Man lives in his states of consciousness, moves and has his being in them.

Whatever our nature is, we did not create it, we can only use it. As ignorance of the law excuses no one from its effects, and as we are all ignorant of our true natures, we are all bound by this ignorance. This bondage is not an eternal verity, yet it is an actual fact. Enlightenment alone can produce freedom.

The eternal inquiry concerning God is an inquiry into the nature of our own being. It is certain that we have a body, and it is certain that we have a conscious intelligence else this page could neither have been written nor now read. It is demonstrable that the body and mind did not create themselves but have their source in Something greater than they are. Hence we are threefold beings, consisting of body, mind, and spirit.

Now the body itself, evolved through untold ages of time and stages of development, must have started somewhere, somehow, with an original concept which man did not create. This original concept must have been an idea in the Mind of God, hence it must be a Divine idea and Divine ideas must be perfect. Therefore it follows that whatever the true idea of body is, or shall be discovered to be, it must be perfect. As yet we do not understand this perfection, although we dimly sense it. In such degree as the mind senses this perfection the body responds to this spiritual awareness and becomes harmonious.

This is not a matter of creation on the part of the individual mind, but is an awakening. All evolution is an awakening and development to a greater possibility, resulting in an unfoldment of an inherent potential. Since man lives in his consciousness, it follows that a change of consciousness will produce a change in outward manifestation. Hence we arrive at the idea that man lives in and by his beliefs and opinions, and that, could he change these beliefs and opinions, there would be an outward manifestation corresponding to the inner change.

A theory basic to effective prayer and Science of Mind is that in reality we are *now* perfect, even as God is perfect, and that this perfection appears outwardly in a ratio corresponding to our spiritual perceptions. We have reached that place in the evolution of our consciousness where the mind begins to grasp a higher order of being. We do not know what the future holds in store, but that it has a new order for humanity there can be no doubt. The old order is rapidly passing and millions of people today are endeavoring to sense their relationship to the Universal. The persistent study of man's nature carried on through the last one hundred years has developed an understanding of truths which will completely revolutionize not only human thought, but its corresponding reactions. Never before has there been such an inquiry as is now being carried on. We are gradually shifting our mental concepts from a material to a spiritual basis. The time will come when all people will look upon humanity as individual incarnations of the universal Spirit, which is God.

The nearer we approach this position, the more we shall withdraw from a false concept of our own being. Man is a spiritual being, using the Law of Mind, living in a world of objective form, and being surrounded by an unfoldment in his experience which is the counterpart of his persistent pattern of thought.

Like produces like. "Do men gather grapes of thorns?" Man's nature is drawn from that universal Nature which is not only the sum total of all individual life but which is also the essence of Life Itself. This ultimate and intelligent Causation is what we mean when we say "God."

That there is a direct relationship between the Universal and the individual there can be no doubt, and that man is the product of the Universal no man can deny. That God or the First Cause is complete and perfect all thinking people have affirmed. Intuition, revelation, and investigation combine to prove the fundamental premise that the First

Cause is complete within Itself, and that we have access to It through our understanding.

The entire evolution of man is the result of gradual awakening to truths which have eternal existence. Evolution is not a cause but an effect. The cause of evolution is Intelligence, the effect is manifestation. As man's body is part of the one great body of all physical life, so is his mind one with the infinite Mind. From this infinite Mind he draws inspiration, knowledge, and wisdom—the direct revelation of Reality through him.

There are numerous channels by which he has access to this infinite Mind. Intuition is the direct inner perception of Truth, while science, by careful investigation, works its way back through appearance to ascertain the cause. However, each discovers a universe of order governed by immutable laws. How could man either perceive intuitively or investigate scientifically unless his consciousness were already *one* with that which it conceives or understands?

The advance made in human progress, through the acquisition of greater truths, is a continual proclamation of the spirit in man as it penetrates more deeply into the nature of that Being which spreads the evidence of Itself throughout all creation and proclaims the exactness of Its Law. The higher discoveries in science have led man to a point which transcends all material form and then arrives at ultimate conclusions, even through pure mathematics, announcing that all movement, all creation, even every creative act, starts with an original unit which is pure Spirit or absolute Intelligence.

3 ·

Recognize Your Individuality

To be an individual means to exist as an entity. Rightly understood, God can be considered as the infinite Person; hence Spirit is the infinite Essence of all individuality. Within the One Supreme Mind, since It is infinite, exists the possibility of projecting limitless expressions of Itself; but since the Infinite is infinite, each expression of Itself is unique and different from any other expression. Thus the Infinite is never divided but has infinite manifestations.

While all people have the same origin, no two are alike except in ultimate Essence. One God and Father of us all, but numberless sonships. Each sonship is unique in a universe of Wholeness. Man is an individualized center of God-consciousness and spiritual Power, as complete as he knows himself to be, and he knows himself only as he really comprehends his relationship to the Whole.

Our individuality externalizes as personality at the circumference of our existence and experience. At the center of our being is the point of individual contact with the infinite Source, of the unexpressed and unconditioned, the Absolute, God. There is a reservoir of life and power as we approach the center which is loosed and flows through to the circumference when we realize the unity of the Whole and our relationship to It. God is incarnated in all men and individualized through all creation without loss to Himself.

Each of us, as a unique individualization of the Infinite, is complete. No two people look alike, act alike, or think alike. No two faces have the same expression. Our fingerprints are different. The emotional reactions of each are distinct and individual. All this, in order that individuality may not be lost in the great shuffle of life. God would not be a creative God if His creations were monotonous repetitions.

The more completely we recognize our individuality, the more unique Our personality. Due to this we commonly speak of persons as being "individuals." A psychological reaction against our machine age is an instinctive gesture of a person protesting against anything that would seek to replace the necessity of more fully expressing his individuality.

As we seek to develop our personalities we should at the same time try to unify them with all others.

Some find their approach to expressing the Reality at the center of their being through art, science, or literature, some others through prayer and meditation; but all do it by extended recognition and increased inner awareness. The voice of the Spirit speaks to and through all; it is a universal language speaking through many tongues.

Emerson tells us to watch the spark which illuminates our own consciousness. This spark is shot from the central fires of the universe and gathers brilliancy within us as we fan it with our awareness of it.

Individuality is the thing behind our personality. Personality is what we make of our individuality. The uniqueness of our personality springs from our individuality, which is entirely God-given.

We think of Jesus, the "wayshower," as a divinely inspired personality, a teacher of man, a lover of humanity, and a spiritual genius. The conscious knowledge of God which impregnated the mind of the man Jesus we think of as Christ, or Christ-consciousness. To worship this personality is idolatry, to believe that God gave more of Himself to this man than to other men is superstition, to think that the word of Jesus had the power to change the natural order of Reality or refute natural laws is ignorance.

As other men, Jesus was a human being, but he was a spiritual genius. Just as we have had geniuses in every field of endeavor, so we have had spiritual geniuses, those who have seen more deeply into Causation than others. Jesus, as a personality, has long since passed to other fields of activity, but the conscious knowledge of God which endowed this unique man with what may be called the Christ-consciousness, remains as a potentiality for all of us.

We are beginning to understand more of the meaning of this Christ, this Emmanuel or God-with-us, the direct relationship of the Universal to the particular, of the Infinite to the finite, of God to man, of the heavenly Father to the earthly son. The forming of this Christ within us is the incarnation of the Almighty, consciously received, and the power attending this new birth is the result of opening a greater channel in our own minds through which the originating Cause may flow.

The greatest teaching of Jesus was the necessity of belief or faith. What should we believe in and how can we have faith? His answer: Believe in God or the universal Spirit; have faith that your belief in this universal Spirit will produce a definite and tangible result in your experience.

It seems impossible to have belief or faith while we doubt or are afraid. Hence the enemies to be overcome are our denials of the good, the beautiful, and the true. "To err is human," and that part of us which is human seemingly is continuously in error, is fearful, timid, uncertain; it needs and must have knowledge of a new source of freedom.

The only possible "salvation" is for a new birth to take place in the mind; it is the mind that needs to be reborn to a greater recognition of the Divinity within it. Hence we are told to be "transformed by the renewing of the mind." The mind must shake off the adversary which is the denial of good, and, looking upward, must become impregnated with the great affirmations of Life Itself.

4 ·

The Law of Your Life

As we approach a consideration of Science of Mind in relationship to our daily living we need not consider it as being deep, abstract, or probably beyond our ability to fully understand. Although it necessarily is founded on great truths, at the same time it is very simple. All too often we tend to complicate our thoughts and ideas rather than keeping them simple and usable.

Let us remember as we progress to keep our minds open to new ideas and be ready to accept old ideas which have been shorn of their worn-out cloaks. We want to be happy and willing to learn more about ourselves, to discover more of that Life of which we are a part, and at the same time to ascertain the nature of the Law through which It makes It-self manifest.

We do live in a spiritual universe, a universe that is intelligent and creative, and it is a thing of law and order. It is God's universe, a Divine idea and thought that has become manifest, God becoming that which He has created through the Law of His nature. It is one stupendous Whole, with God as both cause and effect. Idea and manifestation, and the Law by which one becomes the other, are all one in the inherent nature of God.

Man is an individualized center of God-conscious life, a point in the infinite sea of life, and an intelligent, self-knowing point. Man is the outcome of God's desire to express Himself as individuality. The whole meaning of experience is to promote this individuality and thus to provide a fuller channel for the expression of the supreme Spirit of the universe.

We note that through the ages people have been healed by the prayer of faith, which is a practice of every religion. There is a Law governing this possibility else it never could happen. It is the business of Science of Mind to view the facts, evaluate the causes, and in so doing provide a definite knowledge of the Law which governs the facts.

The universal Mind contains all knowledge. It is the potential ultimate of all things. To It all things are possible. To us as much is possible as we can conceive, according to Law.

Should all the wisdom of the Universal be poured over us we should yet receive only that which we are ready to understand. This is why some draw one type of knowledge and some another and all from the same Source—the Source of all knowledge. The scientist discovers the principle of his science, the artist embodies the spirit of his art, the saint draws spiritual awareness into his being, all because they have courted the particular presence of some definite concept. Each state of consciousness taps the same Source but has a different receptivity. Each receives what he asks for, according to his ability to embody. In this way the Universal is infinite, the possibility of differentiating is limitless.

We waste much time in arguing over things that cannot be answered. When we have arrived at the ultimate, *that is the ultimate*; it is the way the thing works. Therefore we have a right to say that there is a Law involved and that this Law executes our word or prayer. We discover laws, find out how they work, and then begin to use them. Therefore we say it is the nature of thought and of creative Law *to be this way*.

I would say that Law is an attribute of God. God did not make Law; It co-exists with the Eternal. The infinite Law and the infinite Intelligence are but two sides of the infinite Unity; one balances the other and they are the great personal and impersonal principles in the universe. Evolution is the out-working of that which is tangible and mechanical, and involution is the in-working of the conscious and the volitional.

We can no more do without religion than we can do without food, shelter, or clothing. Indeed, the religious instinct is so firmly implanted that it is inseparable from life and living. According to our belief in God will be our estimate of life here and hereafter. To believe in a God of vengeance is one thing, but to believe in a God of Love and a just Law of Cause and Effect is another.

We live in a universe of Spirit and of Law. From the one we are to draw inspiration, from the other we are to utilize power. Each is a complement to the other and both are necessary to existence.

To believe in a just Law of Cause and Effect, carrying with it a punishment or a reward, is to believe in righteousness. To believe in eternal damnation for any soul is to believe in an infinite monstrosity, contradicting the integrity of the universe, and repudiating any eternal loving-kindness inherent in God.

To feel that we suffer for our mistakes is justice, but to feel that our mistakes are eternal is to be already in the suppositional hell of a false theology. A sin is a mistake, a mistake is a sin; both will ultimately be done away with.

To believe that evil draws as great benefits as goodness from the storehouse of God is unthinkable, and to feel that some are foredoomed forever to be evil is also unthinkable. It denies solidarity to the universe and creates a house eternally divided against itself.

All Truth is our truth. No man robs us of our own soul, and our spirit is already one with the eternal Goodness. Everyman's belief is good insofar as it is in line with Reality. We have no controversies with anyone. As we claim freedom, so we extend its privileges to everyone else; we will give and accept on no other terms.

We study the thought of the ages and are not ashamed to admit any falsity in our own thought. We are after the Truth and shall be satisfied with nothing less than that Truth which proves Itself to be really true. We are scientific searchers for that Truth which makes man free, and we know that we have found entrance to It.

The past is behind and whatever doubt it may have held is gone with it. The future is before, bright with prospects; the eternal sun of righteousness is ever ascending, never to descend. Let us look toward the high goal of lasting attainment, fearless and happy. Let us live in the present, looking neither backward in horror, nor forward with apprehension, but looking into the present with joy—"abiding in faith."

5 ·

Prayer Is a Science

There are too many instances on record of a direct answer to prayer to discount the fact. Prayers have been answered directly, specifically, immediately. We are confronted with a fact and not with a theory. We are not seeking to find facts with which to prove some theory, but rather to find a correct theory which fits the facts.

Prayer has been answered in many thousands of cases; the answer has either been through the caprice of some deity, or through the action of some definite law. It is unthinkable to suppose that God, the Creator of all life, gives to some while withholding from others. We cannot believe that God is pleased with some and displeased with others. So we must believe that prayer is answered according to law, and that should we discover the right use of this law, all our prayers would be answered.

What does one do when he prays? *He talks to God.* Where does he talk to God? He talks to God in his own mind, through his own thought or feeling. It is quite impossible for one to talk to God outside himself, for he cannot go outside himself. Whatever God he talks to is in his own thought or approached through his own thinking, feeling, and knowing.

The man, then, who asks God for abundance, asks God in his own mind. God answers through his affairs. But some have asked God for money for some worthy purpose and have not received an answer to their prayers. Indeed, to be perfectly truthful, can we suppose that God is or can be more interested in one good deed than in another? This would be dangerously near making the Divine Being more limited in thought than we are.

But the fact remains that many men's prayers relative to worthy purposes have been answered. It must be that *the answer to prayer is in the prayer when it is prayed* and not in the inclination or the disinclination of God to answer some and not others. God answers prayer according to law and order, the immutable Law and Order of the universe.

Prayer is a thought, a belief, a feeling, arising within the mind of the one praying. This feeling becomes a complete belief and a perfect acceptance when the mind is most completely in tune with the Infinite. The mind is the most completely in tune with the Infinite when the emotions are the most constructively aroused. The highest faith comes from the greatest spiritual awareness.

The prayer of faith is answered because the prayer of faith admits of an answer while the prayer of unbelief does not admit of one. Perfect faith is an unqualified acceptance of the desired result; and this acceptance is a mental attitude which cannot be shaken by any objective evidence to the contrary. The prayer of faith looks through the apparent condition to a perfect fulfillment. Prayer is a mental attitude aspiring toward God as the great Giver of all. Faith is the acceptance that God has given or is now giving. Prayer and faith are both mental attitudes. A continual prayer of faith repudiates all that contradicts the desired end and culminates in positive acceptance.

When prayer removes distrust and doubt and enters the field of mental certainty, it becomes faith and the universe is built on faith.

The mind will soar to new heights when fired by a potent constructive emotion. This explains why people with high spiritual emotions generally receive the most direct answers to their prayers. It matters not what stimulates the emotion so long as it is constructive and agrees with its ideal. The intellect is a cold thing and a merely intellectual idea will never stimulate thought in the same manner that a spiritual idea does.

It so happens, or the universe is so organized, that it is quite impossible for us to arouse the highest emotions and the most creative ones without using the highest ideals. These ideals are always what we call religious or spiritual. But spirituality and religion are not to be thought of as either unnatural or supernatural. Spirituality means dependence on the Spirit. Religion concerns beliefs in God. Both are normal and quite natural to the average person.

God gives some more than others because some accept more than others. The Divine Giver Himself knows nothing about size. Prayer should build up a greater acceptance of God's Life, Truth, and Action, and when it does the response will be commensurate with the higher acceptance. When the whole emotion is aroused and the mental acceptance is complete, the answer will be certain. The Law has not changed, but has responded in a different way.

In an effort to discover more fully the nature of prayer, it becomes a matter of finding out more about the processes of thought and emotion which are the ingredients of prayer. In order to do this it is a case of ascertaining the nature of mind in action, which easily and quickly resolves itself into a science of mind.

The Basis of Science of Mind

S cience of Mind in its broadest and truest sense includes all there is in science, religion, and philosophy. Science of Mind is not a personal opinion, nor is it a special revelation. It is the result of the best thought of the ages. It borrows much of its light from others, but in so doing does not rob anyone, for Truth is universal and never personal. We need the entire revelation of the whole world, and even with this we shall have little enough.

The universe is impersonal. It gives alike to all. It is no respecter of persons. It values each alike. The philosopher, the priest, and the professor, the humanitarian and the empire builder, all have caught some gleam of the eternal glory and each has spoken in his own tongue that language which is, of itself, universal.

Science is a knowledge of facts that are provable. *Science is not opinion but knowledge;* a demonstrable truth of which there may be a practical application. Science reveals universal truths and gives them to the world as practical values and usable facts.

Science of Mind does not scoff at the words or works of medical science, for instance. They both work to help and heal humanity. Science of Mind is a complement to medical science and when so understood and practiced will help heal the world of its physical infirmities. The world of knowledge needs to be knit together and not pulled apart. We have no objection to any form of healing. What we insist on is that there can be no *permanent* healing of the body without a correspondingly permanent poise in the mental and emotional life. Psychosomatic medicine has shown that mental disturbances, conscious or subjective, produce physical reactions in the body. If the body is to be permanently well one's mental life must be creative, peaceful, and happy. This is the purpose of any mental healing, whether it be approached from the psychological or the metaphysical angle. Psychology and metaphysics are but two ends of the same thing; they meet somewhere in consciousness and merge into a perfect unit.

Science of Mind teaches that there is a favorable physical reaction, an effect, which follows a pattern of thought incorporating ideas of health, for the Law of Cause and Effect governs everything. Similarly, it is held that right thinking will result in a greater experience of success and abundance. A successful man thinks success and the Law of Mind that reacts has no other choice than to produce an effect corresponding to the causative idea.

The road to freedom lies, not through mysteries or occult performances, but through the intelligent use of natural forces and laws. The Law of Mind is a natural law in the spiritual world. We need not ask why this is so. There can be no reason given as to why the Truth is true. We do not create laws and principles but discover and make use of them. Let us accept this position relative to the Law of Mind and Spirit and see what we can do with It rather than how we may contradict the inevitable. Our mind and spirit is our echo of the "Eternal Thing" Itself, and the sooner we discover this fact the sooner we shall be made free and happy.

God, the universal Life-force and Energy running through everything, is an intelligent Presence pervading all space; a beginningless and endless Eternity of eternities; a self-existent Cause; a perfect Unit, and a complete Wholeness.

The unthinking would believe that God is a Spirit who keeps books and checks up on the wrongdoings of each individual member of the human race, and that He sends some to heaven and some to hell and all for His glory. Each, according to his own light, has believed in the kind of God who best fitted his personal ideas, or in the idea of God that has been imposed upon him by ignorant or superstitious leaders.

But ever there has been the voice of those crying in the wilderness of superstition, ignorance, doubt, and fear; the voice of those who have thought the thing through to conclusions that have been independent of race beliefs, of the subtleties of religious dogma, and of theological superstitions. These have been the wayshowers of humanity and millions have lighted candles from their flames. But the world progresses slowly; evolution and the growth of knowledge and wisdom is a process of time and experience.

In olden times an intelligent few understood much deeper truths than were known by the multitude, but the common people were thrown a few crumbs from the tables of those who were "in the know." These crumbs were shrouded in mystery, symbol, word picture, and parable. Perhaps this was the only way in which wisdom could have been taught at all.

In principle the great religions of the world do not differ as much as they appear to. Stripped of their accumulations of adornments and observances, and incrustations of interpretations, it is found that each acknowledges that there is one central Power, Force, or God, which is Self-existent; and it is from this One Power that all things emanate. All of life flows from It and is a part of It. Nothing can exist separate from It. The Christian interpretation of the ultimate nature of the creative Source of the universe places more emphasis on the life of the individual as being an integral part of the One Life. For this reason an intelligent understanding of the fundamental concepts of Christianity has had a greater appeal to the progressive peoples of the world.

But even in the Christian religion much of its real meaning is hidden by words that are misleading and symbols that but few understand. We could scarcely find a greater riddle to solve than the meaning of the "Holy Trinity." Also, most people either reject the Bible entirely or accept it totally and literally. Both these methods are mistakes.

Religion is a man's idea of God and the Bible is a written declaration of the belief in God held by a great race of people—the Jews. It is, in many respects, the greatest book ever written and does truly point a way to eternal values. But it is only one explanation and cannot be considered the only light on religion; for there are many others, which, taken together, weave the story of Truth into a complete and unified pattern.

The many sacred books of the East constitute other Bibles which point ways to the Truth; but each is only another way and cannot be considered to be *the way*. All races have had their religions and have had their Bibles; all have pointed a way to ultimate values, but can we say that any of them has really pointed *the way?* It is unreasonable to suppose that any one person or race encompasses all the Truth and alone can reveal the way of life for all others. This viewpoint does not apply to other forms of knowledge but seems to be adopted only when dealing with religion, and it is a great mistake.

The world is tired of mysteries, does not understand symbols, and longs for Reality. What is the Truth? Where may It be found? and how used? These are the questions that an intelligent person asks and he must have an answer. He may find his answer in the study of Science of Mind. Shorn of dogmatism, freed from superstition, open at the top for greater illumination, unbound and unlimited, Science of Mind offers the student of life the most understandable and intelligent approach that the world has so far achieved.

Intellectual freedom and religious liberty are necessary to the unfolding spirit in man. Whatever is true is free to all alike. We cannot cover the Infinite with a finite blanket. It refuses to be concealed. God has no favorites and knows no privileged class.

Science of Mind reads everyman's Bible and gleans the

truths contained therein. It studies all peoples' knowledge and draws from each that which is self-evident. Only that which is self-evident can stand the test of reason and time. Without criticism, without judgment, but by true discrimination, that which is true and provable may be discovered and put to practical use.

We should take truth wherever we find it, making it our very own. Borrowing knowledge of Reality from all sources, taking the best from every study, Science of Mind brings together the highest enlightenment of the ages.

PART TWO

Growing from Fear into Freedom

Ever since the first cell of life appeared on this planet there has been a continual upward spiral of growth and development. The many manifest forms of life appear to have had a purposive directive factor behind them. This directive factor seems to have had a culmination in man, and even man in his present physical state no doubt will still have future refinements.

We have discovered much about the physical aspects of living things, but about that apparently unique phenomenon in man—his mind—we still have much to learn. What it is, what it can do, and the potentialities latent in it are hardly yet recognized. However, the appearance of mind in man, the ability to think, is the most recent and the culminative expression of the purposive action of Life.

It would appear that for the most part man is still in his infancy in developing the use of his mind. Mind has been given to us, but what happens to its growth and development is largely an individual undertaking—ours is the responsibility to use it and unleash its limitless possibilities. It is in our proper use of the potentialities of the mind that rests our power to release ourselves from fear and discover a new freedom for expressing and experiencing that greater joy of living which is rightfully ours.

7 ·

Unlimited Growth

The history of man is a record of the awakening of the self to the Self, the emergence of the universal Spirit through the individual mind. It is as though we had been pushed from the Center of all things and must make the return journey through self-discovery. The greatest lesson in spiritual education ever taught—the story of the Prodigal Son—was given to illustrate this idea.

Man's primal existence was originally an idea within the universal Mind which became individualized as man. Man expresses through personality, possesses free will, for the end purpose that he may choose to return to "the Father's house." Then he no longer is just an expression of God but becomes a *copartner* with the Infinite. He still is subject to the laws of love and of reason, but at the same time is dependently independent; that is, dependent on the Universal but independent in It.

We should deeply ponder the significance of this thought, for it gives the assurance that our future evolution will not be by compulsion but by cooperation. "For the earnest expectation of the creature waiteth for the manifestation of the sons of God." The whole history of human evolution proves this position. Natural forces undreamed of in previous ages are, today, a part of every man's experience; and since we cannot have exhausted the Infinite, we must conclude that the future holds undreamed of things for us.

It is significant to remember that since the first man turned his face from the clod, rose to his feet and proclaimed "I am," the universe has silently awaited his conscious cooperation with it. This awakening has ever found its starting point in mental states, or modes of thought. *It is the mind that awakes.*

From the dawn of human history until today this inner awareness has produced a steady and unbroken sequence of accomplishment and progress, and while there have been periods when this evolution appeared to stop or to be broken, it has always started fresh and new. Glancing back over the whole panorama of human existence we cannot fail to see a steady advance. Looking, then, into the possibility inherent in the future and judging the future by the past, we cannot fail to see the necessity of eternal progress.

The natural order of evolution has brought us to a place where there is a quickening of the spirit, a keener perception of the mind, a deeper introspection of the soul; the veil between Spirit and matter is thinning. We are emerging into a spiritual universe, proclaimed alike by the philosopher, the religionist, the scientist, and the idealist, and yet the nature of Reality or ultimate Truth cannot have changed. Two and two were four a million years ago. The awakening is to the mind and spirit, and from this mental and spiritual awakening follow objective equivalents.

As the last one hundred years has witnessed the unfoldment of the physical sciences through the consciousness of man, so has it witnessed a great awakening of the mind to itself. The passing of old orders of thought is but a proclamation of the inauguration of new and higher orders. The unravelings of psychology, the birth of modern metaphysics, the enlarging of religious concepts, the inquiry into philosophic problems, all announce a new birth of the mind, a new discovery of the self, a new consciousness of the intimacy of the mind with the subtle Spirit within.

We shall never know any God greater than the God which our inner consciousness proclaims, for the reason that this inner proclamation is "the Father in us." That Silent

Voice, that Divine Urge, that insistent demand made upon our minds, is the original Spirit. The impulse back of our constructive acts is the original creative Genius of the universe flowing through the channels of inner perception in our own minds. Within us this Cause, perennial in Its eternal youth, is ever born anew into creation.

There appears to be one persistent purpose behind the great forward movement of evolution, namely, the outpush of Intelligence, through creation, into higher, finer, and more complex forms. This is one great lesson which science teaches us—that there is an insistent and intelligent Urge in the Life-Principle which impels It to express, and theoretically we might add that It expresses in order that It may become conscious of Itself in many forms.

Theoretically, then, we may believe that the Spirit is forever clothing Itself in form; it is not only Its desire to do this, but by very reason of Its nature It *must* take form. If we were to ask our imagination why this is so, the answer might be that God Himself would remain a nonentity unless He were expressed; that even to the Infinite some form of creative action and expression is necessary.

If we were to further inquire of our imagination what the ultimate purpose of evolution is, the most logical answer it could give would be that the purpose of Life is to produce beings who can consciously cooperate with It; that through such cooperation the evolving Principle Itself may more completely express.

Turning from fancy to fact, we find the facts fitting nicely into the fancy. We feel justified in starting with the assumption that all creation exists for the purpose of spiritual Self-expression; and that man, the apex of creation on this planet, has already reached a place in his evolution where he may consciously cooperate with the Creator.

What the God-intended man may be no one knows, but judging the possibility of man's future evolution by his past, we may rightly suppose that this possibility reaches out and on into limitless fields of self-expression. Man as we now know him is incomplete, and those vague feelings and subtle senses of interior awareness which arise within him are gentle but persistent prophecies of still greater achievements.

The path of progress seems to be persistent and must be eternal; we cannot doubt that the God-intended man will fulfill the most cherished desire of our imagination. It is not of great importance to man's future what processes he may have gone through to arrive at his present place, although it is of great interest and of scientific value to know of his development from the first form of life to his present state. The real problem that now confronts us is not what we once may have been, but, *where do we go from here?*

Man is a self-conscious, individualized center of volition,

will, and choice merged into personality. The more deeply we penetrate his nature, the more significant becomes the meaning of that nature. It seems fathomless, boundless, and almost entirely unexplored. If we start with the theory of an infinite potential latent within him—that he has already reached a point in his development where his own conscious determination must, to a great degree, measure the possibilities of his future unfoldment—we shall recognize this most significant fact: Our future progress depends upon our ability to consciously cooperate with nature and its laws and consciously identify ourselves with the Spirit of Intelligence animating nature.

There is an inner urge in our own minds to grow, to expand, to break down the barriers of previous limitations and to ever widen our experience. This persistent urge is a Divine influence, an irresistible force, and constitutes the greatest impulse in human experience. Mostly misinterpreted and misunderstood, and often pursuing devious pathways, it is still the urge back of all accomplishment, the promise of all fulfillment.

There is this question, however, which naturally rises: Why all the suffering, sorrow, and pain; why has tragedy accompanied the journey of man? Again our imagination may answer this question in a somewhat plausible manner.

There is no other way through which true individuality can evolve. Man must be let alone to discover himself, else be compelled, arbitrarily, to follow one road, in which case he would be an automaton and not an individual. Perhaps this will solve the whole problem of evil in human experience and at the same time point to a better way—that of learning to consciously cooperate with nature and its laws. This the scientist is already learning to do. This the religionist must also learn to do. Life is not really against us but *for us*, for we cannot imagine a universe divided against itself; but ignorance of law excuses no one from its effects.

We are now equipped with sufficient intelligence to gain the necessary knowledge for our future growth. We must free ourselves from superstition, fear, and uncertainty, and ever seek the inner guidance of that intelligent Purposefulness which has already projected Itself into our form and into our creative imagination. Listening deeply to this inner Revealer, we shall find our footsteps more and more continuously guided.

We are beneficiaries of the Universal, or if we wish to state it another way, "sons of God," and that sustaining Infinite, that originating Cause, that Divine Intelligence which has brought us to this point is to be trusted, but we must learn how to make our thought receptive to It. Thus shall we learn to take part in creating our own destiny, to rejoice in the accomplishment already made, and to look forward to a future bright with hope, filled with limitless possibilities, animated by Divine purposes, coordinated by a sustaining Unity, illumined by an eternal Presence of intelligence, wisdom, and right action.

8.

Think Constructively

Thoughts are things. This sounds familiar enough; we have all read it many times. But if this is true why can we not think and, through thinking, get what we want? We have been told that we do not get what we ask for because we ask amiss. All this seems very confusing for we also have been led to believe that we should receive anything asked for if we ask believing. It must be that some ideas are more potent than others, that some thoughts have more power than other thoughts, and this is actually the situation.

All thought is creative, but the real constructive creative power of mind comes only from *true* thoughts. True, positive, and affirmative thought has *real* power, for it produces the correct answer. Negative thought also has power for it produces undesired conditions. When we place a positive thought beside a negative one, when we recognize the beneficial one and understand the nature of the harmful one, then it is that we find that the true constructive idea can dominate and have complete power over the destructive one. Thus it is that we are told to know the truth if we are to be made free.

Thoughts are things. Yes, true thoughts are true things, false thoughts are false things. If we think according to the nature of the Divine, then shall we get what we want? Yes, provided what we wish for is *really* the truth. No, if it is not really the truth. We can never get five by adding two and two although we might believe that we can.

But how are we to know what thoughts to think? What should be the content of our prayers and spiritual mind treatments? How are we to know the false from the true? The answer is more simple than it may appear. Goodness is the truth, and so is beauty and strength and life and love and abundance and loyalty. Even the apparently selfish desires of our hearts are true if they do not contradict the fundamental Truth of the universe, which is unity and goodness and purity.

Our difficulty is not great provided we keep a few fundamentals in view. We have a Divine right to all that makes for a happy life. Abundance must be the heritage of our Divine nature. Our life must come from Life, and peace and happiness cannot contradict Reality. We shall not pray amiss if we affirm these things as part of our experience. Therefore, if we ask, believing, according to the Law of our being we *must* receive.

What we wish for and need is peace, ability, happiness, harmony, plenty, and a greater degree of livingness together with love and beauty. Possessing these we should be in heaven and we ought to be in heaven here and now in our daily living; that is, we should be in harmony with Life. There is no Power in the universe which wishes to withhold good from us—let us forever wipe this idea off the slate of our minds. God is eternal Goodness, hence no evil need befall us either here or hereafter. Life cannot produce death, consequently we cannot die even though we pass through the experience miscalled death.

But what is there left to ask for? Nothing. We need but to *accept* and make use of that which already is and *is for us*. But each shall individualize the gifts of Life through his own nature, and this individualization constitutes that activity which personifies through each of us—the eternal Mind of the universe. This is the play of Life upon Itself and the desire to express which is working through all of us. There can be no life without living, no creator without a creation. And there can be no satisfied man without an adequate expression. There is nothing wrong about desire provided desire is in harmony with Truth. A man who has no desires is asleep and needs to be awakened.

What then if we should desire some special thing that we might enjoy it for a season? Can there be anything wrong with this? Certainly not if this desire harms no one and helps us to express. If, then, we desire some special thing, why should we not ask for and receive it? But how do we ask? *By knowing in our own minds that that for which we ask we now have.* This creates the image of our desire and makes a definite pattern through which the energies of Mind may intelligently and lawfully act, and to which there may be attracted the conditions necessary for the fulfillment of the desire. And according to our belief, receptivity, and full acceptance will it be done.

We cannot live by proxy or attain by pretense. We are dealing with real laws and actual forces when we deal with mental and spiritual laws, and they cannot be fooled. From our own endeavor will come our own reward, only now we know that we are dealing with a Law which is amply able to fulfill the rightful demands made on It and which is intelligent enough to always bring them to pass. With this in mind we shall do our spiritual mind treatment work gladly and cheerfully and with much less effort, for we are no longer struggling against Life but flowing along with It. We are going with the current and not against it.

We should feel equal to any occasion and be overcome by none. We should enter any and all true endeavors with a zest for the game and get a real joy out of living.

9

The Potentials of Thought

In defining consciousness we find it impossible to conceive of an unconscious state of being, just as it is impossible for one to conceive of oneself as dead, or as not having being. Consciousness, then, is not only the starting point of perception, it runs through all perception and without it there can be no real perceiver.

To really define consciousness seems difficult, yet we all know what the word means for we are conscious beings and cannot imagine ourselves to be in other than conscious states. The movement of any particular state of awareness is a movement of consciousness. The movement of thought is a movement of consciousness.

Prayer, meditation, hope, fear, doubt, all are states of

consciousness. To the individual nothing moves unless consciousness is aware of the movement, for if there is a movement without any consciousness to be aware of it, then that movement is without reality, so far as we are concerned.

There is movement in the universe; however we are only partially conscious of many of the movements. These movements and their meanings we but imperfectly understand. The whole history of the human race is a history of the unfolding of consciousness. It is no wonder that many have said that whatever a man can become conscious of he can understand or accomplish. Let us consider what it signifies to *really* become conscious of anything, for it is more than a mere claim, more than an affirmation.

When a child is told that two and two make four, his consciousness begins to work on this problem; he becomes aware of the fact that two and two are four. At first this fact seems external—he must have four blocks laid before him, must be told that one block and one more block make two blocks—that two and two make four. He now understands that four is a real number, having an actual significance in his everyday life. As he becomes really conscious of what four means, he no longer needs to have four blocks laid before him for he is conscious of four without the symbol. He is now inwardly aware. He is now completely conscious of a new idea. It is his. He cannot be robbed of this knowledge for it is a part of him. He becomes partially conscious of the significance of numbers.

If, however, we confront the same child with higher mathematics, we find that he is unable to understand. He has not yet become aware or capable of understanding more advanced knowledge. But it does not follow that he will never become conscious of greater realms of mathematics for he already has a starting point. Thus it is with life and action. We all have a starting point—our mind, our consciousness—and from this point all must travel. The advance in science, art, literature, and all endeavor is an outward and then an inward swing of consciousness. What we can become aware of we can master, and since no man can set any limit to the "measure of man's mind" there can be no limit other than the confines we set ourselves.

That there is a Mind in the universe which is without limit seems a true deduction. That we have access to this Mind seems the only explanation of our ability to progress. That we must be one with this Mind is an inevitable conclusion, else how could we perceive anything at all? That inquiry into any truth is some working of this Mind through our consciousness is apparent, and that all progress is the unfolding of this Mind through our consciousness is the only explanation for our continual progress. That this Mind is a storehouse of untold possibilities we cannot doubt, and that the greatest possibilities of our future lie in the direction of our conscious unity with infinite Intelligence we cannot deny.

A man sits down to write a play, his thought conceives of characters and their actions. The play is in his mind else there is no play. He creates the characters from his thoughts and gives them the only life they have or ever will have. The play is real to another man only when the author's thought is tangibly projected into the visible world. The other man, however, cannot know the play unless he becomes conscious of it, and even though he sees the play actually performed, the only meaning it has to him is that which his thought gives to it.

We are still mostly unconscious of what the great minds have thought, even though we know what they have said. Our own consciousness must supply the only interpretation we can have. If the thinking is deep and we think deeply, the ideas and meanings take on a new color. Our consciousness is striking deeper and deeper. We are more and more aware of the subtle meanings of the great man's mind. We are becoming consciously one with him. A unity is being made and our own consciousness is now an outlet for his. So it must be in our relationship with the great Mind.

Reality is forever hidden from our view. We see, not Life,

but that which lives; not Energy, but that which Energy becomes; not Mind, but that which Mind does; not the Creator, but creation. Who ever saw the Power that guides the stars through space, or grasped in his hand the Energy that balances a spinning top? No man has seen God at any time. No man has seen man—the real man—at any time.

We are forever dealing with forces the only evidence of which is the use that we make of them, and we do not think it strange. Why then do we think it strange that there should be power within man himself? Is it not man's mind, the invisible agent, that discovers *external* evidence of power? What if man should discover a power within, more subtle but equally as potent as any of the powers of science which have been harnessed and caused to do his will? Such a power he *has discovered*, but it cannot be analyzed! It must be accepted. This is why we are told that we must live by faith.

This inner power comes not with a blast of trumpets nor a glare of lights. It has been truly said that the pen is more mighty than the sword. Yet the sword has laid low countless hosts, destroyed nations, and established despots in power. But after the sword has been corroded by rust and bent in shame, the words of power—Truth—have lived and conquered and destroyed all enemies. The nearer we approach the Truth the more power we have. Why? Because this is the way of Truth. What is this power? Our consciousness of the Allness of Good, our perception that God is supreme. Where do we perceive this? Within our own minds and hearts.

How much good and how much power can a man perceive? As much as he can believe in and really understand. No man has ever, as yet, plumbed the depths of his own mind and no man ever will, for here is a deep which cannot be fathomed, a height which cannot be scaled, a breadth which cannot be spanned. No wonder Shakespeare said, "To thine own self be true." The self is a hidden reservoir, fed by a stream whose source rises in the Infinite. The Infinite appears to continuously flow out, and the Source and Its flow are one.

Our life's source is the Infinite. The flow through us equals our receptivity to this source. We did not place this Power within us and in the long run we cannot misplace It. Browning speaks of this as a spark which a man may desecrate but which he can never quite lose; and Shakespeare, as that "divinity which shapes our ends," while Jesus speaks of it as the kingdom of heaven within.

There are certain things which we must accept and one of these is that we all have an *inner power*. But let not the boastful brag nor the braggart boast—*the source is the Infinite* and our inner life is forever wedded to It. The still, small voice within proclaims itself only through a consciousness of this unity, and this unity become a power to us only through the good use made of it. Power is silent and deep, calm and undisturbed. Tennyson says that when the outer tempest roars, this inner life has power to walk the waters.

Now since our inner power arises only through our unity with God we approach it only in the desire for good, never in willing evil. Since this inner life is one of unity we cannot approach it while we have a sense of separateness. And since God is really the life of man, man has real power only in such degree as he first recognizes his unity with God.

Who can say what a man might be able to do if he were really in league with the Spirit of Truth, really in touch with his true self? The reward which we have reason to believe in is certainly worth the effort, which effort is a peaceful approach to Reality. And there should be nothing peculiar in the process. Simplicity forever accompanies true greatness, and directness is the shortest distance between two points. One point is the human, the other the Divine. There is nothing between except what we put there. We are too apt to approach Reality by indirection and thus become confused by the shadows of our own misunderstandings.

Again, let our approach be simple and direct. All the statements ever penned by the hand of man will avail nothing if our inner sense of Reality be lacking. A statement is not the way, it is simply a pointer, a guidepost. No man's prayers can be better than yours. No man's shadow can reach any farther than the one you yourself cast. Loose the self, and let the wise follow their own wisdom, but see to it that *you* follow the direct path of your own soul straight to the center of your own life, which is God.

Direct the Energy of Thought

I t is unthinkable to believe in a God who creates man only to set him adrift in a nothingness, burdened with care, doubt, and uncertainty—destined eventually to go to a suppositional hell because he does not know enough to go to an equally suppositional heaven. If we believe in a God who creates man out of Himself, we must believe that since this God has intelligence enough to make man, He has resources enough to provide for his well-being.

We are, we think, move, and act. We observe everywhere the intelligent phenomena of some Cause. This presupposes the necessity of an underlying Intelligence. Nature lies in the lap of an Intelligence and Life, which, without any apparent effort on Its own part, provides both seedtime and harvest.

How, then, can we doubt that the Power back of things is adequate and is a Unit?

Originality, consciousness, spontaneity, and volition are evident at every turn in the road of human experience, making it unreasonable to hold a materialistic concept of life. There is but one plausible conclusion that back of everything, coordinating everything, unifying everything, is a unitary Power, all-knowing, all-wise, all-good, all-beautiful, absolute, birthless, deathless, and changeless.

Our popular religions, with their half-gods, are but different resting places of the mind—inns where the weary soul rests overnight on its journey from the extreme outer circumference of materialism to the inner consciousness of spiritual Reality. In the morning of a greater vision, with the dew of Eternity on the grass of experience, the soul ventures forth to find a better God.

Our half-concepts come *as* we need them and remain *while* we need them, to be finally drowned in a greater concept of Reality. Everyman's religion is good for him though it may seem inadequate to others. Religion has ever been an answer to the cry of the soul for something which is real, something which may be relied upon—a resting place for which every person instinctively feels a need.

We are created, we are told, in the likeness of the Eternal, after the image of the Infinite. We sense a Divinity within, a nature hidden in the cryptic interior of our minds which we have scarcely penetrated—a unity with the Whole. The intuitive faculty which we use to uncover Reality is evidence that this Reality is already latent within us.

It matters not if we reach this place through the inductive process of science or through the deductive process of revelation. It is useless for the materialist to say that revelation is a myth, for it can be shown that science is an inductive process leading to deductions, and that all deductions are revelations. All life is a revelation from the cradle to the grave. By revelation is meant the uncovering of that which *already is*, but is new to us.

The most penetrating and far-reaching conclusions ever made by man have announced that creation is a result of the Self-contemplation of God. The Law of the universe propels Mind into action, action into creation—creation being an effect, a result. The creative word of universal Intelligence projects itself into form. When we speak of the energy back of thought, or the power of faith and prayer, we are not thinking of will power, but of original Power. The thought, or the prayer, merely uses an energy which already is. The scientist does not put energy into electricity; he takes it out.

If there is a law of thought, if there is evidence that any prayer was ever answered or that any man's faith has consummated in an objective realization of that faith, then there is evidence of an Intelligence in the universe which accepts the word of faith and acts upon it.

An intelligent person approaches prayer knowing that there is a universal Law which acts on his word, and he uses this Law with the definite knowledge that he is scientifically using a proved principle, a known, definite, and provable force. For to him the presence of an intelligent Law in the universe, which receives the impress of his thought and acts upon it, is an accepted and proved fact.

He also knows, however, that this Law can only respond by correspondence. In other words, the measure of our faith in the Infinite is the measure of our capacity to draw from the Infinite. This is why the Great Teacher said that it is done unto us as we believe. If one can believe in a great good, then that much good can come to him. It is according to our mental acceptance or mental equivalent—according to our faith— that Life manifests through and for us.

Man measures life through his concepts. Automatically, thought has power. If one wishes to demonstrate a spiritual Principle which he may lay hold of and definitely use, let him forego any sense of coercion and become as a little child in receptivity; let him definitely and consciously accept his good and continue accepting until he experiences it. We must subject ourselves to the Law if we wish the Law to subject Itself to us. A good-natured flexibility with oneself and a faith, persisting in the face of anything which would contradict it, is the only way to approach the Principle of right action.

Deep within our minds is the Spirit, which we but slightly comprehend. From this universal reservoir a Power of spiritual consciousness passes through our minds into action. When the mind is peaceful and still it catches a vision of this greater good. While the mind is in turmoil and conflict it cannot receive an image beyond the vicious circle of that small measure in which it has been treading around. Somewhere the walls of the measure must be broken down. We must learn that we can transcend our previous experiences; that we are bigger than we know; that beyond the finite is the Infinite.

We will never arrive at the point of demonstration—experiencing the intended purpose of our prayer—while we believe we have to put energy into Spirit, thus usurping the throne of the original Creative Genius. There is a certain faith to which even our most materialistic scientists find themselves as subject in their realms as we shall ever be in the realms of Mind and Spirit. There is an energy in thought, not because we wish it to be so, but because it is so. Definite and specific thinking draws this energy through our conscious desires and makes manifest these desires at the level of our comprehension of Good.

There must be a conscious belief on the part of the one seeking to demonstrate this principle that his faith and thought are but the avenues through which the Law expresses Itself for him. In the technique of spiritual mind treatment, thought merely uses the Power intelligently. The will is the ability to select a specific thought thus determining how the Power is to be used. Well enough to realize that there is an infinite Intelligence back of everything, but if we have a problem to solve we must *know* that this infinite Intelligence is *now* solving it. This is to be remembered when giving a spiritual mind treatment. The treatment should be concrete, specific, conscious, definite, embodying the general ideas which one wishes to have become part of his experience.

While there is a point of decision and choice in treatment, there must be no outline. If the treatment is the cause, the demonstration is the effect and is already in the cause, as the flower is in the seed. It is written: "I am Alpha and Omega...." Treatment should be given definitely and consciously, with a complete acceptance that there is a Power, an Intelligence, a Law which operates upon our word. Whatever the mind holds which denies this acceptance should be specifically attacked and consciously neutralized. The mind must be cleared of doubt and left open to accept the effect of the newly created cause.

Any experience which proves to a person that his faith

can loose an intelligent Power which responds to him will
be more salutary in his life than all the knowledge of what
the sages of the ages have written. One definite experience
which proves the integrity of a man's spirit and its direct
relationship to the universal Mind and Spirit will do more
for the individual than to know all the teachings of theology.
For thus alone can he arrive at the place where he can say:
"I know, that, whereas I was blind, now I see."

The energy back of constructive thought is Spirit. Spirit
permeates everything. Hence constructive thought calls the
best out of any particular experience. One who uses the Science of Mind is a practical idealist, but not a dreamer. While
there is in the innermost recesses of our soul a place which
dwells in eternal stillness and inaction, there is also a place
at the circumference of our being, which, animated by the
inner Spirit, goes forth to accomplish. Thus alone can contemplation become fruition, and inner recognition outer
realization.

An unexpressed man is incomplete, and the objective
universe through which alone we interpret the invisible
Cause is evidence enough that the original Creative Genius
forever passes from formless Energy, through Law, into
manifestation. We would defeat the very purpose of life
should we live in a continuous state of meditation or prayer,
oblivious to the objective world. The practical values of

spiritual perception remain latent until objectified. Any attempt to isolate oneself from the world of action is contrary to the order of the universe, hence futile. The practical religionist seeks to make his dreams come true, and, unless his dreams are subjective hallucinations, they will become actual experiences if he demonstrates his principle.

The average man may spend fifteen minutes to an hour each day in meditation, but this amount of time is of inestimable value in his practical life, for it is here that he joins the ideal to the real, receives inspiration for action and guidance toward accomplishment. In actual practice he tries to sense the union of the Spirit with everything he is doing. His slightest desire is important to the universe since it is some expression of the Parent Mind through him. This gives a dignity to his slightest undertaking and places a greater value on human endeavors. The happiness of the individual life is essential to the universal Wholeness, for thus alone can It find an extension of Itself.

The one seeking to demonstrate the power of spiritual mind treatment in everyday affairs should think of himself as being divinely guided. He affirms that his mind is continually impressed with the images of right action, and that everything in his life is controlled by love, harmony, and peace; that everything he does prospers, and that the eternal Energy back of all things animates everything he undertakes.

He should resolutely deny every objective evidence to the contrary and in its place there should come a sense of right action. He should feel within him a unity with the Spirit, with the Spirit in all people and running through all events. He should definitely declare that the spirit within him is the Spirit of God quickening into right action everything he touches, bringing the best out of all his experiences, forever guiding and sustaining. The greatest good which his mind is able to conceive should be affirmed as a part of his everyday experience. From such daily meditation he should venture forth into a life of action with the will to do, the determination to be, and a joy in becoming.

Practical Thinking

We all wish for better health, greater happiness, and a larger experience in living. There is a Spirit *in* us which desires to be more fully expressed *through* us. This Spirit is conscious Life as opposed to, or different from, Law and Its mechanical action. Man's consciousness of his own existence is the Self-recognition of the Spirit within him.

We do not see this Spirit but we feel Its presence and we see Its manifestations in all our actions; without It we could neither act nor be conscious of ourselves or of anything else. In reality man's spirit is his share of that universal Presence in which all live, move, and have their being, hence the spirit of man is the Spirit of God in man—the two are really one and it is this inner Spirit which wishes to become more fully expressed through us. The *action* of the Spirit, flowing through our mentalities, is the Law of our life.

To use Science of Mind successfully one should be conscious of the indwelling Spirit operating through his own thought, will, and purpose. He should realize that the movement of his consciousness of God in and through him is a reality. Apart from the One Knower there is no knowledge, and separated from the One Life there is no real living.

Man's mind is ever in contact with Omniscience, but his conscious thought does not always know this. Hence he remains in ignorance of that which he inwardly and subjectively knows, but does not bring to the point of consciousness. One should feel that the inner Spirit knows, and that, because this is true, one's objective mind knows. In this way he is led into the right paths of human activity, for *human activity, rightly conceived, is Divine.*

There is but One Knower and what this One knows must be and is so, and this is true when this One knows through what we call the mind of man. The question might arise at this point: "Suppose man should know something which contradicts the Truth?" The answer would be: "Man cannot really *know* anything that contradicts the Truth." He may *suppose* something which is not true; he can *assume* an opposite to Reality, but he cannot *know* that which is not so. For instance, we might believe that two and two make five, but they would still make four. There is a great difference between believing and knowing; we can *believe* anything, we can *know* only that which is true.

Our troubles come, not from wrong knowing, but from wrong believing; they are misconceptions about what is true. One of the intellectual difficulties which we must over-come is our apparent inability to realize that there is an ul-timate Truth and this Truth operates through our own mind in Its native and original being and power. But our percep-tion of the Truth is an act of consciousness, as it is the inner perception which must recognize the Spirit.

In practice we start with this premise: The Truth is and is perfect, wherever we find It; being omnipresent It is where we are, where everyone is, and in and through all things. God is *in* and *through* His creation and the creation of God, rightly viewed, must be perfect.

The sum total of human knowledge comes to us through some avenue of the self-knowing faculties. We gain knowl-edge through science, opinion, and intuition. Science is the result of careful investigation and tabulation of facts, causes, and conditions. Much, but not all, of our knowledge is ac-quired in this manner. Intuition is a direct perception of the knowing faculty, without data, procedure, or any process of reasoning whatsoever. Our greatest truths come through this avenue. Opinions are our personal ideas about that which intuition gathers and science guarantees. Opinion is the least of the avenues of knowledge.

It is interesting to observe at this point that while the real intuitive perceptions of the ages have remained unchanged and are unchallenged by any ideas to the contrary, opinions are in a constant state of flux. This does not invalidate the findings of science nor overlook the value of opinions. Of course the *principles* of any science, rightly interpreted, cannot change because they are based on immutable laws and laws do not come and go, they are eternal verities and may be absolutely relied upon. As scientific research with its continual new evidence draws us nearer and nearer to basic Reality, our opinions change to meet the new facts and our intuition is opened to receive newer and greater truths. Thus do the three paths to knowledge combine to lead us on to a greater good.

The highest opinions of the deepest thinkers of all ages have agreed that we live in a spiritual universe governed by exact laws. A true philosophic outlook by science will not contradict this position, and the intuitive faculty, when clearly operative, will add its testimony to the same fact.

The spiritual universe is an intelligent organization bespeaking a universal Intelligence running through everything. Our own intelligence perceives this as an ultimate necessity and when our intelligence perceives it as an ever-present fact, we are practicing Science of Mind. The practice of Science of Mind, then, is the exercise of the knowing faculties of the mind functioning on the plane of self-recognition, and must ever be considered from this viewpoint.

It is impossible to separate the mental from the spiritual. The two are one. God is spiritual awareness, whether we think of this awareness as in the mind of man or in the infinite reaches of the universal Mind. The Truth is not broken into fragments but remains as one unitary Wholeness.

In the application of Science of Mind one should be aware that he is using original Divine Power and that he is using It as definite Law. It is not the law of *his* mind but the Law of the *One Mind*, and this should not be forgotten. He should not feel that he is compelling any reluctant power to do his bidding, but that he is using a natural law in a normal way. The practical use of Science of Mind is a spontaneous recognition of the ever-present Spirit. And deep spiritual awareness does give one a greater ability to heal and to help.

Spiritual mind treatment requires a belief on the part of the individual that the words of his treatment are law unto that to which they are directed, then he should act as though his belief were true. He does this in a perfectly normal way, starting with the premise that Spirit is a universal and perfect Presence, filling all space, molding every creation, and animating every form with intelligent energy. Spirit is the intelligent Life-Principle running through all.

One needs to seek a sense of the perfection of the Divine Presence and to substitute this knowing for ideas of disease, poverty, or discord. In doing this he must often confront negative thoughts with the declaration that there is no necessity for the continuance of a condition contrary to fundamental Good. When the objective belief *in* and the subjective image *of* any given trouble is neutralized by the realization of Good, the condition is met and a healing takes place.

There is nothing which can hinder Law from working. It is never a question of how much the Law will work, but always of how well we can use It. We can constructively use It to the degree our thought and belief will let us, no farther, but always *as far*. The Principle is infinite, but we are only as capable as we know ourselves to be; we can know ourselves to be capable only insofar as we are unified with Truth. Thus does the impersonal become personal.

Spiritual mind treatment, prayer, is more than an act of the intellect; it is an act of one's whole being, a complete giving of oneself to the realization of Perfection as being an ever-present fact in everyday experience. It carries with it a spiritual sense which cannot be put into words but which must be *felt*.

The thought and the intellect have a definite and a necessary function in spiritual mind treatment, but the final effect, of necessity, must and can only be the result of an *inner realization* that is stronger than the belief which caused the disease or discord. Conviction reaches its own level just as water does. This is a natural law in the spiritual world. All laws are natural, and all causes are spiritual.

To be spiritually minded is our natural impulsion toward Reality; it is normal, and should be spontaneous. To be spiritually minded is to believe in the Presence of Spirit and to trust in Its intelligent response to us in accord with Law. Spirit is but another name for Life. To be spiritually minded, then, is to completely believe in Life and in the responsiveness of Life to the aspiration of the human soul.

We should ever endeavor to sense this universal Presence, and time should be spent in bringing our consciousness to this recognition, for this is the Power that heals and remolds according to a more Divine pattern. Whenever we contact any objective evidence which denies the perfect Presence and the perfect Law we should consider it as an appearance only and not as a part of Reality.

Remember that *thoughts are things*, and that an idea can be erased by denial or by the affirmation of another idea. We must ever strive to cause our thought to rise above the level which produced the discord we seek to heal if we are to be successful in spiritual mind treatment. We will always find that insofar as we do recognize the perfect and the harmonious it will appear, no matter what the evidence to the contrary may be.

Again we are brought back to the fundamental principle of Science of Mind: God is, is Perfect, and is *All*. We should know that behind every manifestation there is the essence of Perfection, which, although it may not now appear, can be permitted to flow through it. We need to go beyond the physical vision, clarify the mind, and purge subjective concepts. Insofar as we are able to do this the rewards of our spiritual mind treatment will be certain. Behind the apparent is the *real*, and when this *real* is sensed the apparent more nearly measures up to it.

To successfully use prayer, or spiritual mind treatment, we do not withdraw from life but enter into all legitimate human activities with enthusiasm, realizing that the Law fundamental to all creation should give joy in the everyday affairs of life. The humble is exalted, each thing has its place in the Divine order, and the expression of happiness in the individual life is as essential to the Divine Being as is the manifestation of the glories of the heavens surrounding us.

In the vast panorama of life we behold the eternal Energy

of Mind set in motion through Divine imagery and manifesting Itself in all creation. Thus, and thus alone, is the Spirit manifest on this or any other plane. The budding rose, the flowering tree, the corn ripe for harvest, the child at play, the surging tide, the saint kneeling before the altar of his faith, are all manifestations of the One Life, One Presence, One Power.

The Power of Right Thinking

The power of our prayer, thought, spiritual mind treatment, is only equal to our conviction of the Truth, our embodiment of Reality, and our unconditioned reliance upon Good. Having accepted the proposition that we are not only immersed in a sea of living and creative Intelligence, but that this original Cause flows through our own minds into new creations, it naturally follows that we should examine our thought to see what we are really believing in.

If the original Mind can flow through us only at the level of our acceptances of Life, which seems certain, then our acceptances of Life automatically decide what is going to happen to us. Clear thinking converts the mind, revitalizes the consciousness, readjusts our valuations, and gives us a new outlook on life. We no longer ask what is the possibility of life, but we seek to determine the nature of our thinking. How much do we think we can achieve? How much abundance can we mentally embody? How much health and happiness can we conceive of? And how great is our faith that our prayer will become our experience? We find that for the most part we have set severe limitations upon ourselves, so we should readjust our thinking to a more positive, affirmative pattern that accepts a greater portion of the limitless good that Life is ever ready to extend to us.

Just as there are laws of matter, so there are laws of mind, for what is true on one plane is true on all. This, no thinking person can deny. If certain factors in physics produce certain results, then certain mental factors will produce certain results. This is a field for exploration and experiment as yet almost entirely untouched; and yet in the laboratory of mind lies a possibility of research as fascinating as that in the laboratory of matter, with undreamed of potentials awaiting discovery.

If we mix the concept of good with the concept of evil, the result will fluctuate between the two. If we mix a concept of peace with one of confusion, the result will be both peace and confusion. If our thought fluctuates, our external world will fluctuate also. Suppose we should try this experiment with ourself, saying: I am now convinced that the ultimate

Power is Goodness. I am equally convinced that anything in my present experience which is not of the nature of this Goodness is the result of misconceptions on my own part. Furthermore, I am convinced that through the reversal of my thought and the changing of my concepts my whole external life can be rebuilt, re-created. From now on I only affirm the positive; and disclaim and repudiate, but not combat, the negative. I shall no longer resist evil, but I shall embody only good which overcomes all unlike it. I have neither enemy nor enmity; I shall entertain neither in my thought. There is nothing working against me. Everything is for me and all apparent contradictions to this Truth shall vanish as the mist before the sun.

This mental position would be an experiment in thought, in mind. We would not go through life blindfolded; we would not be declaring that evil is good; not merely saying peace when there is no peace thus hypnotizing ourself by our own suggestion, which is an error we must be very careful to avoid. But we would be demonstrating that an active consciousness of good overcomes evil. This anyone can do who is convinced that the power of right thought is actual and real.

We cannot expect to convert our whole consciousness in a moment, nor is it necessary. But if we take the mental stand that evil and negative conditions are not things in themselves, and constantly and consistently affirm that good alone has constructive and lasting power, is a spiritual entity, and has a real Law to support it, and that good *is* active in our experience, then we will demonstrate our theory, no matter what the existing conditions to the contrary may be.

We must not balance good against evil but must replace, overpower evil by the presence of greater good. In Science of Mind we start with the proposition that pure Spirit, or absolute Intelligence, is perfect Life and perfect Law; that this Intelligence flows through us at the level of our comprehension of It; that clear thinking creates within us an embodiment of this good, which embodiment automatically projects itself into form in our experience. We must know that we are dealing with a Law which need not be coerced but which must be used, and that the conscious use of the Law produces definite results.

The results will be as definite as our consciousness of them, since the Law flows directly through our consciousness manifesting the results. How careful, then, we should be not to mix conflicting concepts in our consciousness, not to become confused by objective situations. We work in our own mind and there re-create the condition, establish a new mental concept of the condition as it should rightly be, leaving the projection of this new creation entirely in the hands of the Law. And if we ask: How can anything be brought into being? or, What is behind all creation, our own lives and experiences included? how can the answer fall short of the proposition that the initial movement of creation starts in pure and positive Intelligence, unconditioned by any external fact?

This pure and original Cause, this absolute Intelligence which is the initial starting point of *all* creation, must be as present in Its entirety *now* as It ever was or ever can be. It must start as fresh through our minds as It did in that supposed dim and distant past when the Primordial Word spoke Itself into being. Creation is not a finished product but an eternal emanation. All life is an effect, a way, an outward manifestation of interior causes, silently working within themselves and shaping things at last to fit the Divine mandate.

Insofar as our thought rises to a realization that creation is an internal process projecting itself *now* through our minds, working through our thought, positive, original, invincible, shall we see why it is that right thinking has power.

Probably the greatest single determining factor of our experience in living is what we think. Whether it be a matter of health, supply, happiness, success, harmonious relationships, or any other aspect of our life, in and behind it is the causative, creative pattern of our thought.

Freedom from what we do not want, and our emergence into a life that is more complete with all those things which contribute to the welfare and happiness of ourselves and others, would seem to depend on to what extent we are able to consistently control, guide, and direct our thinking.

Once such a start is made, regardless of how meager it may be, it is a foundation upon which we may build, until the time comes that we know with a confidence and a surety that when a particular constructive thought is entertained in mind there will definitely follow a tangible manifestation of that thought in our daily living.

To be able to accomplish this rests in understanding and using our minds in a specific manner. There is no formula to follow, but there is a technique to be acquired.

13

Mind in Creative Action

Whether the mind is in the body or the body in the mind, no one knows. No one knows what the ultimate of matter is, but that it is a formless energy seems to be the generally accepted theory. That this energy takes tangible form throughout all creation is obvious. Form is necessary to the expression of the Spirit, and without body or form It would remain unexpressed.

Theoretically we believe that Spirit, acting through Law upon some cosmic Energy, takes definite form for the purpose of Self-expression. The mechanical processes involved are not essential in a philosophic discussion; hence we view the matter from the standpoint of cause and effect, leaving the ways, the methods, and the means to a more intricate analysis by the scientific mind.

It seems evident that form is the result of some purposiveness in the universe, some force acting creatively through law, the result of which is the evolution of form or the physical universe. This concept has always been held and is continually referred to in most of the sacred writings. In the Christian Scriptures we find such expressions as "in the beginning was the Word" and "all things were made by him" and "the Word was made flesh." There comes from antiquity a system of thought, which has been more or less adhered to throughout the ages, teaching that the pure essence of Intelligence, Spirit, or the Absolute, is the one *reality;* that all nature is a reflection of Its ideas, and that all nature has no other source.

Plotinus, considered to have been one of the greatest thinkers of all time, expressed the idea that nature is the great *no thing* yet it is not exactly *nothing,* since it is its business to receive the forms which the Spirit imparts to it. Some current-day religious groups, harking back to this teaching of antiquity, misinterpret its meaning and proclaim the utter unreality of matter and mistakenly conclude that the physical universe is an illusion. Now the physical universe is not an illusion, although some may conceive it to be such. Plotinus implied that nature is no thing of itself—it lives by proxy, it is the projection of That which is something. But it does have a definite purpose: the expression of the Spirit in tangible ways and in a concrete manner.

To look upon matter as an illusion would be as great a mistake as looking upon it as a thing of itself. The tangible world thus becomes a mirror in which is reflected the countless forms of the Divine and Infinite imagery which we ascribe to the Spirit. The Absolute and the relative are not opposites, each is a complement of the other. We cannot have an Absolute without a relative; we cannot have a relative unless there is an Absolute; they are two aspects of the same thing, one is cause and the other effect.

To suppose that that which is created governs that which creates it is to fall into error. To suppose that the Creator is absorbed in His creation is equally an error. To believe, however, that creation is saturated with the essence of the Creator seems reasonable, and that there is a certain immanence of the Creator running through all nature seems reasonable also. No fact is isolated, *no form can be isolated from the Principle which creates and sustains everything.*

In the mirror of the objective universe we behold the marvelous manifestations of a subtle, invisible Mind or Spirit, and as we enter into communion with Its innumerable forms we are, through them, communing with Spirit Itself.

Forms come and go, but the creative Principle remains intact. The Spirit Itself knows no time, yet all times must be included within It. It knows neither large nor small, as size, yet all form is known to It. If we can learn to supply the material object with a spiritual significance nature will more completely stand open to us—it will not be an illusion but a sublime and a necessary conclusion.

Our conscious, constructive use of the Law of Mind exists to us only as a latent possibility until we specialize It. The declaration that It exists and that we believe in Its possibilities is merely a statement of principles, a proclamation of our faith in the responsiveness of the Spirit to the needs of man; but a proclamation of faith never built a house or drove an automobile. "Faith without works is dead."

The Law of Mind is to be consciously used, definitely specialized. When we have freed ourselves from superstitions regarding spiritual things we shall be ready to approach them intelligently and incorporate them in our everyday living. We should daily seek to do this in our use of Science of Mind. We have a creative intelligence so we should use it. We are surrounded by a spiritual Principle of Law that reacts to our thought so we should consciously avail ourselves of It for definite purposes. Spiritual mind treatment is the act, the art, and the science of specializing the universal Law of Mind for specific and individual problems.

The Law is, but It must be used. Until the time comes when we use this Law consciously and constructively we shall be using It unconsciously and perhaps destructively, for every time we think, we use this Law. We should begin by weeding out all negative states of thought and learn to speak a straight affirmative language. The Universal gives to us through us.

To believe that one is continuously guided in his acts by a supreme Intelligence is a better state of mind and more productive of good than to believe that one is subject to the caprice of fate. Our fate is within our own minds. Destiny is but the objective manifestation of mental states. Success and failure are not things of themselves, they are simply modes of expressing the Original Thing. Thought should be daily directed and consciously controlled.

It is written that God's words are "yea and amen," which means that the Infinite does not argue but meets every man's approach directly, always responding by acquiescence to every man's thought. The physical scientist readily acknowledges a reign of law. The forces of nature are not coerced, they are directed; so the powers of Mind and Spirit need not be commanded but commandeered. They are not reluctant; they are willing. The Universal flow is forever taking place; the turning of this flow into the channels of constructive thought is an individual act.

The simplest approach is always the most direct—believe and it shall be done. Accept and let it be done; convince the mind and no longer deny the greater possibility. "Act as though I am and I will be." We must abandon our ideas to the supreme Cause and wait for the harvesttime with joyful expectancy.

There should be a definite and conscious expectancy. We should feel as though the entire power of the Spirit is for us and never against us. All ideas to the contrary must be resolutely set aside. Remember that spiritual mind treatment is neither wishing nor willing, it is an affirmation of the presence, the power, and the willingness of the Divine to specialize Itself for us, to meet every human need, to heal our bodies, to intelligently guide us, and to bring success into our undertakings. It is not through human determination, not "by power or by might," but by the silent workings of the Spirit through our organized thought that the Divine imparts of Its power to man. We are chemists in the laboratory of the Infinite; what shall we produce?

14

The Technique of Science of Mind

A spiritual mind treatment is an act of the mind consciously conceiving the presence of some desired good which one has not before experienced. The principle involved is based on the theory that we are surrounded by a universal Law—a creative medium which is receptive to our thought and acts upon it automatically in an intelligent manner. Consequently, a treatment is the formulating of our thought in such a way as to bring the attention of the mind to the realization of harmony or health, of happiness or success, depending upon the result desired.

It is a fundamental proposition that the universe is a perfect unit and is always in harmony with itself. God is never divided against God; harmony is real, eternal, fundamentally necessary and true. A spiritual mind treatment must inform the mind that whatever appears wrong is entirely an appearance, a misjudgment, or a false conclusion. We do not say the fact does not exist. For instance, we do not say a man is not sick, but rather this: If he can succeed in unifying his thought with Life he will be healed. We do not say a man is not unhappy, but we do affirm this: If he can succeed in uniting his thought with That which must be happy, with eternal Happiness, he will be happy. We may say he is poor and needy, but if he can unite his thought with That which cannot be poor or needy, he will cease being poor and needy.

We do not deny the evidence of any experience because experience is the only means by which we may affirm that we live at all, for without experience there can be no life. We do emphatically state that any experience which is less than harmonious, less than the Eternal Fact, is an unnecessary condition. We experience discord because we wander away from Harmony; we experience limitation because our thought denies Abundance.

Now I am aware that an unthinking individual first hearing of this is liable to say, "Well, that sounds foolish. It sounds very foolish to say that by the act of thinking you can produce anything in the visible world." But if this same individual will pause for a moment and ask himself, "Where would I be, or what would happen if I, the thinker, were not here?" he would at once realize that nothing could happen to him. The moment you take the thinker away there is nothing left, and if we could disjoin the universe from the Intelligence permeating it there would be no universe.

Our inner belief decides what is going to happen to us, but that belief is the result of much ignorance and needs to be enlightened; hence the necessity of meditation, of prayer, of spiritual mind treatment. A prayer or spiritual mind treatment is a conscious, definite centering of thought on some desire, uniting this desire with ultimate Reality, causing the mind to perceive that this universal Reality is forming Itself through the pattern of the thought or desire.

We should not deny ourselves the right to do this, and if we subject ourselves to the necessary conditions we will prove it! The right mental conditions or concepts are these: The universe is a perfect Unit; life is One; at the root all is One; it is many in the objective world because Unity or Oneness manifests in multiplicity differentiating Itself in variety. That which is One becomes many, but the many are still rooted in the One, without which they could not be. It is necessary then that the thought unite with the One, that is, it must recognize but One Power back of everything.

Since there is but One Power back of everything, whatever exists is this Power in some form, whether we call it good or bad. Hence we are healed by the very Law which

makes us sick. If we believe that everything is wrong, everything will appear wrong and the Law will see to it that everywhere we turn things will be wrong. If we can bring our
consciousness to a place where everything is conceived as
fundamentally good and we perceive only harmony, we shall
ultimately experience only that which is harmonious. Each
lives unto himself and unto the Unity behind all things.

It is necessary that we recognize the Unity, Harmony, and
Power back of all things, and then state that It is operative
wherever and on whatever our thought rests. That is what a
treatment does. A treatment thus becomes a spiritual entity,
equipped with volition, propulsion, action, and a complete
knowledge of how to manifest itself. No one knows why this
is so, but it is so.

There is in the treatment just exactly as much and no
more than we put into it. I do not mean put into it by force,
by will, or by any compulsion, but by absolute conviction,
by positive affirmation, by complete acceptance, and by true
receptivity. The treatment is the nucleus, the seed, the idea
around which the energies of Spirit play, just as the creative
forces of the soil, sun, and air take the seed and produce a
plant. So spiritual mind treatment is a concept through
which universal Law flows, producing a form like the idea
given It, just as the ground always gives us back a plant
which is the logical outcome of the seed placed in the soil.

We involve the seed; nature evolves the plant. We involve the idea; the spiritual Power which surrounds us, operating on this idea, evolves the thing. But as we can only harvest what we plant, we can only take out of our garden what we put into it, so a spiritual mind treatment can only produce its logical correspondent.

It is necessary in giving a treatment to dissolve, within our thought, everything which denies the word that we speak. Nothing can neutralize our word but ourselves. When our word is spoken in harmony with the Truth it is linked with the inmutable Law of the universe. Hence a treatment seeks only to convince one's own mentality and never tries to convince anyone else.

In giving a treatment you are not holding thoughts, you are trying to convince yourself of the presence and the reality of the condition which you wish to bring forth. Always your treatment begins and ends within yourself, no matter what your word is spoken for. Because you are dealing with an intelligent Law, when you specify to yourself what your word is for the Law executes the word at the level of your recognition and acceptance of it.

We are surrounded by a receptive and creative medium which receives our thought and acts upon it. This is proved and may be announced as a definite principle. Because this is true our thought decides what is going to happen to us.

Were we ever so religious, ever so desirous of doing right, and should still think destructively, we would be subject to destruction. The Law is an unfeeling thing, just as is the law of electricity, which will just as quickly electrocute a saint as a criminal because it neither knows nor cares about saints and criminals. The Law says this: "Here I am; you can never get away from me." "As a man thinketh in his heart, so is he."

It is not going to do any good to say, "There is nothing but plenty in the universe," and then go out and talk poverty. The Law is always right here and says, "Here I am. I am an immutable fact. I am an eternal presence. When you say 'Yes' I say 'Yes' and when you say 'No' I say 'No,' and when you say 'It is good' I say 'It is good.'" Or as Jesus said: ". . . as thou hast believed, so be it done unto thee." We must carry the science of our religion into everyday life—everywhere.

There is nothing harder than keeping the thought straight, and nothing else so desirable. It is not easy in our contacts with the daily world to keep our thoughts so clear that we never become unpoised, that we never accept anything which we do not wish to accept, that we always control the intellect so that the emotions cannot respond unless the intellect says to respond. But whenever we can do this our destiny will be in our own hands, backed by an immutable Power. But before we do this we must relate and harmonize ourselves with the Infinite. The Infinite is so constituted that It never fights Itself, hence we must not fight It; but we do fight It when we admit that anyone fights us. We oppose It when we admit that anything opposes us. We deny It when we admit that good is denied to us. The Law always stands by saying, "Here I am, continually reflecting into your experience exactly what you think into me."

We must take the Science of Mind into everyday life, and when we find ourselves confronted by discordant conditions we should never say, "Oh, what's the use, what's the use?" but rather say, "There is Something in me which is greater than this condition and It can dissolve it." We have the privilege and power to do this, and if we use this ability properly it will be productive of salutary results.

How do we do this? Very definitely. Very specifically. Always we bring our conscious thought to bear upon the specific condition which needs to be changed. For instance, if one were treating to heal himself of eye trouble his treatment would be so formulated as to bring out the realization that his vision is a perfect manifestation of a Divine idea. If, on the other hand, one were treating his business for activity, he would bring to his mental attention the realization that right where his business is there is a Divine Law of harmony, of plenty, and of continuous action.

In an iron foundry the liquid metal is poured into different molds and cools off in specific shapes. This is the way a treatment works. It always works from the basis that the cause of everything is an idea and that the thought is the mold into which our tangible experience is cast.

Hence it is necessary that a treatment be specific. All treatments are based upon the same principle but each treatment is a mold with a certain specific form. Consequently, in spiritual mind treatment the ideas incorporated must encompass the entire situation being treated. If the case is one of unhappiness we must make it clear to our consciousness that happiness is *real* and that unhappiness is a condition based upon a false premise. Back of unhappiness is the thought that there is not good enough, love enough, peace enough, health enough, nor understanding enough to go around so that as a result some of us lack or are short of the good things of life.

In the infinite nature of Spirit, and therefore back of everything, there is enough of peace, of good, of health, and of abundance to go around. Convince yourself, explain to yourself, what is wrong and say, "All of the abundance and peace there is is right here and flowing through me. I can no longer be unhappy." In other words, show yourself why you believe what you believe. By expelling or neutralizing false conclusions the newly established right ones will demonstrate themselves. The more completely your consciousness is in harmony with truth, beauty, peace, love, and righteousness the more power it will have.

There is nothing too great or too small for the action of Law. The same Power that swings the planets in space also creates the buttercup and the aroma of the rose. As Emerson said: "There is no great and no small to the Soul that maketh all, and whence it cometh all things are, and it cometh everywhere."

In spiritual mind treatment never try to make things happen, but *know* you are permitting them to happen and *feel* that they are happening. Imagine them to be happening, and during the process of the transition from the point where you are to the point where you would like to be, pay no attention to any discordant things which may occur.

The worse things seem, the more carefully you should go within yourself to declare the reign of God's Perfection. The worse the condition appears, the more certain you must be that you will accept nothing but harmony. This is the attitude that distinguishes the man who *knows* what he is doing in using the Science of Mind from the one who only *hopes* that something will happen. When a gardener goes forth to sow seeds he sows the kind he wants, and if other things come up during the process he uproots them and knows he is going to reap in due season a harvest of the things he has sown. He is working with definite laws. This is the right kind of faith; it is both scientific and practical.

In the use of Science of Mind one knows, with absolute certainty, that he is planting a seed—a constructive thought—in an absolute, causative Principle. When other things come up he says, "Those are the weeds, those are the negative thoughts," and he pulls them up—neutralizes them in his own consciousness. Then gradually that which was once a desire becomes an actual experience. He knows what he is doing, how to do it, and in doing it he realizes that behind and in his present act there is an eternal Intelligence from which he may draw greater and greater inspiration, knowledge, and power.

15

The Rediscovery of Health

The practice of spiritual mind healing is based on the theory that man's life is rooted in Divine Life and that through his mind he has access to the Original Spirit which animates everything. On first thought the possibility of any healing by this method seems rather vague, since both its principle and performance take place in an invisible realm. But, as a matter of fact, the technique of spiritual mind treatment in physical healing is both concrete and specific, for when one stops to consider the proposition he realizes that all causation is invisible. There are certain assumptions or faiths which we must accept in order to proceed with any activity in life. One general faith which all instinctively do accept is that *life* is in all animate things.

The physician to the physical body makes no attempt to create or coerce life; rather, he starts with the assumption that his patient already has life. His entire effort is to keep the body free for the expression of this life. The physician really treats the body as though it were an instrument through which life flows; in doing this he assumes that there is a Life-Principle already existent and perfect, ever striving for an adequate outlet.

The physician may not think of this life as being Spirit; he may call it nature. It makes no difference what he calls it; he knows that when the body is healthy the Life-Principle flows through it freely; and his business is to assist this circulation, to help the body throw off its impurities, to keep it from becoming congested, and to see that there is proper assimilation. When there is proper assimilation, circulation, and elimination, there is physical well-being.

When the physician proceeds in this manner he is cooperating with nature and its laws; he is, in reality, a copartner with the Originating Spirit. All true physicians understand and appreciate this position, and the layman can understand the work of the true physician only from this point of view. With this understanding in mind the spiritual practitioner cannot feel antagonistic toward the work of the medical practitioner.

When we analyze the methods and procedure of the psychiatrist we discover that his fundamental faith or assumption is not unlike that of the physician, for he also starts with the premise that nature is forever expressing itself through us; but the psychiatrist deals not so much with the body as with the mind, basing his work on the theory that many of our human ailments are the direct result of mental disturbances.

A mental disturbance or imbalance generally indicates some inhibited, misdirected, or blocked action in the conscious or subconscious part of the mind. It is the business of the psychiatric practitioner to restore mental equilibrium, with proper assimilation, circulation, and elimination. He is repeating the work of the physical practitioner, the only difference being that he is dealing with the mind directly and the body indirectly.

There should be no confusion between the general practitioner of medicine and the medically trained psychiatrist. One works with the body, the other with the mind, and since the mind and body are now conceded to be so knit together as to be inseparable, it follows that a good doctor of the body also needs to be a good psychiatrist, while a good psychiatrist needs to consider the body as well. The best results are obtained when the physician to the body is also a physician to the mind.

In analyzing the position of the spiritual practitioner we discover that his assumptions and faiths are almost identical with those of the physical and mental practitioners. He also starts with the assumption that life *is* and is forever seeking manifestation, but he calls nature and life God, pure Spirit—the intelligent Life-Essence animating everything.

He also realizes that the body cannot be well while there is poor assimilation, poor circulation, or a lack of elimination, any more than a stagnant pool can be pure; the pool is purified by running water. The spiritual practitioner knows that unless the assimilation, circulation, and elimination are well ordered, the body will become diseased. Hence his position should not be one of antagonism toward the other practitioners but should be one of cooperation.

The field of the spiritual practitioner lies in that realm of thought where pure ideas are introduced into the mind. In this he is a psychiatrist, since he seeks to straighten out his patient's consciousness. But it is not necessary that the spiritual practitioner have a thorough knowledge of human anatomy, medicine, and the variations of the process of thought, although it might be an aid to him if he did have familiarity with such knowledge.

The spiritual practitioner starts with the assumption that God is, and that man's life is rooted in pure Spirit. His whole work is in the field of mind and Spirit; in the field of mind since his treatment is a thing of thought, in the field of Spirit since his thought seeks to rise to a belief in and acceptance of Spirit as being the life of his patient.

The medical practitioner starts with the body; the psychiatric practitioner starts with the mind; and the spiritual practitioner starts with the Spirit. So interrelated are these three that no man can tell where one begins and the other leaves off. We shall understand the whole man only through our consideration of this threefold unity of body, mind, and Spirit.

The spiritual practitioner devotes his entire time and attention to building up a spiritual consciousness, a realization of a Divine Presence within his patient which is pure, perfect, and forever flowing. He seeks to impress upon his own mind that the life of the Spirit—filled with goodness, with peace, with perfection, and with pure being—now permeates, animates, harmonizes, and controls every atom, cell, and function of the person he is treating.

He knows in his own mind that this pure Spirit is forever flowing free and clear and has no congestion or impurities. He further knows that the Original Life-Force is now eliminating from his patient's mind every belief in or experience of anything which would impair or impede the Divine currents. He works in cooperation with both the physical and the psychiatric practitioner, for when the three shall work harmoniously together with one end in view—the well-being of the patient—they shall have arrived at the most effective method yet known for complete healing, for the making of a person whole again in every respect.

16

The Control of Conditions

When we speak of using spiritual mind treatment for correcting undesirable conditions we are not suggesting that any mental or spiritual conjuring trick is involved, nor is the hope being held out that anyone, through imagination, will, or concentration, can bring into his experience that which is unlike himself. For instance, a man who knows nothing about music would be wasting his time visualizing himself as a grand opera singer. We must never forget that in dealing with spiritual and physical laws any energy must conform to the instrument through which it flows. This statement in no way can be construed as contradicting the limitless possibilities of Life nor the potential possibilities of man, but it is evident that whatever the Law does for us must be done through us. Hence it is necessary that we furnish adequate channels, as well as being receptive to It.

The facts involved in the effectiveness of spiritual mind treatment in material affairs are greatly misunderstood. Many believe that by thinking, willing, and wishing, by concentration, meditation, and prayer they can bring into their experience something which is utterly unlike themselves, but such is not the case. Yet it would be a mistake to deny ourselves the privilege of knowing that there is an intelligent Law which is accessible to us and which will react in our favor when we allow It to do so.

In everyone there is a unique possibility ever ready to become an expression of his individuality, and if he has not yet discovered his particular niche in the scheme of things he should work more for direction and guidance than for the fulfillment of some special desire. When the mental gate, which obstructs the flow of Spirit through the uniqueness of our individuality, is lifted, there will be an outpush which nothing can resist. Every man, then, should be willing to be himself, remembering with Emerson that "imitation is suicide."

In our spiritual mind treatments we need to affirm that that which most perfectly expresses us, that which will bring happiness, abundance, and peace into our lives will be made known. A treatment which embodies the idea of good and of abundance and which rests in faith will always be effective. The effective prayer is always "Thy will be done"; but we should know that the Divine can will nothing less than freedom, that limitation and lack must melt before It.

We should think of ourselves as happy and prosperous. The drag of the necessity of any limitation should be neutralized through the recognition of Life indwelling us and springing spontaneously into manifestation through our endeavors. And how can we assume such a mental attitude in honesty, in sincerity, and with conviction unless we are already convinced that whatever the nature of Reality is, it is always for and never against us? If we could sense that our place in the universe is Its expression of Itself through us, we would know that there is neither competition nor monopoly in right action. God makes no bargains and the Principle of our being argues with no man.

The originating Intelligence is a straight affirmation. To be forever fighting conditions and meeting emergencies in our minds is an obstruction to experiencing a greater good. There is a certain Divine freedom manifest throughout all creation, a certain flexibility in nature which we overlook. The Spirit cannot flow in freedom when our thoughts are rigid; then the gates of abundance are closed and our circumstances become cramped.

Unless we can sense a good which we do not see, and believe in a Power greater than our finite efforts, we shall tread around in a vicious circle of unattainment. When we are willing to let go and to receive into our intellects the new stimulus; when we have learned that the Law which creates and maintains all things is inseparable from our own thought, we are ready to demonstrate, and not until then.

When the Master Metaphysician said that *it is done unto us as we believe* he announced the law of mental equivalents. While there is a Power and a Presence in the universe which can and does respond to us, It can only respond *to* us *through* us. The Spirit cannot give that which we are unable to receive. It is infinite, forever flowing, and Its nature is to be always giving of Itself. Our receptivity to and embodiment of It automatically sets the gauge to our demonstration.

Our embodiment of It is more than a mere repetition of words. Anyone could stand in front of a paralyzed man and tell him to arise and walk, but it takes the consciousness of a Christ to know that the man will actually rise and walk. The words used in spiritual mind treatment have a power equal to the conviction behind them. Therefore it follows that a spiritual mind treatment must convince the mind of the one giving it; and, if it is to have any power, must find an embodiment in his mind through which the intelligent

Law is set in motion finding an outlet and establishing a corresponding experience.

We cannot ponder this thought too deeply and everyone practicing Science of Mind should analyze it completely. The mind of man is the universal Mind individualized in and flowing through him. It is the original Creative Genius of the universe finding a fresh outlet through his mind, but how can It find an outlet unless there be first an inlet?

When a person gives a spiritual mind treatment, time is spent in bringing that assurance to his own mind, that conviction in his own thought, and that embodiment in his own spirit which shall thoroughly impregnate his own consciousness with the realization of the presence and the power of an active, intelligent, and creative Agency working through him.

To this universal Agent there can be no limitation. It is the sole and sovereign Agent of the universe and unless one believes this he cannot practice Science of Mind successfully; otherwise he has no principle and no power except that of the human will which always falls in its own tracks and dies for lack of nourishment.

There is no real mind or spiritual force outside of or external to the original Creative Cause. In no way does this make mere puppets of individual minds, but it does limit the activity of these minds—if this can be considered limitation—

to their perception of Reality. There is plenty of freedom, however, in this concept since we are to recognize our own minds as outlets through which the original Mind works through our creative consciousness. Rather than a sense of limitation, this should give us a sense of freedom and unfold in our imagination a transcendent possibility.

The spiritual practioner's work is quiet, within himself. He must remove every sense of limitation from his work, let his word loose as though it were an original Cause, unconditioned by any relative fact. There can be no sense of competition, monopoly, restriction, or existing condition imposed upon his word if it is to have power and effectiveness. So perfect and unified are the instinctive perceptions of his word as a subtle and natural Cause in the spiritual world that the mind cannot conceive of It in fragments or in parts but only in Its wholeness.

Our security lies in this sense of unity and of the inevitable outcome of good. No treatment can have power which supposes an opposite or which seeks through mental coercion to either restrain or compel. Hence it is written: "... not as I will, but as thou wilt." The will of the Infinite can be nothing less than goodness, happiness, and peace. Any denial of a condition in the treatment is for the purpose of eliminating a belief in the necessity of any opposite to the unitary Wholeness which is being proclaimed, to establish in our minds the recognition, the embodiment, and mental equivalent of our highest ideals.

It is impossible to practice this science either scientifically or effectively unless we are willing to subject our thought to this test. If the mind embodies goodness it can speak goodness; if it has an equivalent of peace it can give peace; if it has a sense of abundance it can demonstrate supply. But the moment it falls into the error of mental manipulation it has reduced itself to the level of wishing and willing and its power soon becomes exhausted, the fire dies out, and the ashes of hope lie dead and cold upon the altar of a broken faith.

Abundant Living

The theory that we have the ability to change objective conditions through the creative power of our imagination rests upon the belief that behind the solid fact there is an Intelligence, a formless Energy, and a Law whose nature it is to manifest as form. This theory, coupled with the belief that our minds, our thoughts, are directly related to the infinite guiding and directing Intelligence, is the principle involved in the control of conditions through the creative power of our own mental action.

Experiences in the endeavor to prove this theory justify our acceptance of it. Whether or not we have been as successful as we would like to be in consciously directing our affairs through the creative power of thought, we may still rest assured that any apparent failure may be ascribed to insufficient knowledge of this Principle rather than to Its unwillingness to operate for us.

We should no longer ask ourselves whether or not there is such a Principle, but this: To what extent have we gained the ability to use It? The known laws of physical science will prove of little avail in this matter. Theological speculations are useless and philosophic discussions bear but little fruit. We are facing the problem directly as individuals—*do we or do we not believe?* If we do not have a sufficient faith, how shall we acquire one?

Each man should be the master of his own mental household, although but few are, and "he that ruleth his spirit (is better) than he that taketh a city." The problem is one of *real* belief. If we can sense the fluidic nature of all that has solid form, that Energy becomes tangible according to a pattern, and that the solid form is an effect and not a cause, we shall at once know that in order to demonstrate we must more or less disregard the form and look to the Presence—spiritual Reality, Mind—in which originate the thoughts or ideas for the patterns of all that has form. We are too liable to be awed by the form and to stop at our point of contact with the tangible object. We go so far and no farther, refusing to look beyond to That which created it.

This intellectual obstruction is a lack of spiritual perception, a denial of the Creative Cause, and it results in limitation. The best practice for the conscious control of conditions is not the use of affirmations which declare that the All-Good is omnipresent, but is a quiet assurance in our own minds that the Spirit is both ready and willing to take full charge of our affairs, coupled with a persistent determination to believe that It is doing so.

But in so doing It must flow through our belief and must take the forms which our belief creates. The Spirit cannot give us something we do not accept and this accepting is a mental act. We must cause our minds not only to *believe* but to consciously *receive*, to concretely and definitely *accept*. Hence another proposition follows this one: the mind cannot accept what it rejects. The mind cannot affirm what it continues to deny. A weeding-out process is necessary, an uprooting and replanting, a cultivation of the creative soil of our imagination. The ground must be prepared for the new crop and we must wait patiently upon the Principle of Life to produce the new form. Meanwhile we should be careful lest, through denial, we affirm a belief which is the direct opposite of the good we desire.

The process is really simple. We must refuse to entertain doubts and fears and resolutely set our minds toward faith, acceptance, and receptivity. We must be patient with ourselves when we appear to fail, rejoicing when we conquer. There must be a flexibility of thought as well as a determination of purpose. In spiritual mind treatment we should turn entirely from the undesirable condition, and, looking through it, as it were, see the opposite outcome.

Each undesirable condition must be transmuted into a good one, and we must stretch the imagination to include the more, the greater and better things. Calmly persisting in the maintenance of this mental attitude, we are certain to win.

There can be nothing in the universe operating against our word except our own doubt. The Law cannot, because the Law is impersonal. God cannot, because God is the impulse which causes us to seek to express a greater, fuller life. Hence nothing can neutralize our work except ourselves. Whatever hinders, inhibits, or denies the reality of an omnipresent Good and Its eternal flow to us must definitely be erased from our thought.

We must consciously set the Good in motion, recognize and let It work for us. So long as a certain specific fear comes to our consciousness we should daily meet it, and, looking it squarely in the face, explain to ourselves why we do not need to be afraid of it. We should always be building toward the affirmative side of life, toward the recognition of an eternal and ever-available Goodness in the universe, ever manifesting in our lives and affairs.

A direct application of Science of Mind to the problems

of the business world is both possible and practical. Business is a thing of thought followed by action. Without *thought* there could be no motive for action, and without *action* thought would remain unexpressed. Back of every enterprise there is some mind at work giving it the stimulus of its creative thought. This is a self-evident fact.

Often the mind which creates a business so endows it with vitality that the enterprise sustains itself long after the originating mentality has entered other fields of action. The thought has been so fertile that the business itself has become an entity in the minds of all engaged in it. But once let this mental pattern, this subjective action, cease to be and the business will fall apart like a chain of sand.

Business, like all things on this earth, is not an eternal verity. But, like most of the things with which we deal while in the flesh, it is necessary to the world in which we live. It is not a question of doing away with business, but of making it a success and a thing of joy.

Any activity which does not express a constructive program is wrong in principle and cannot be made right in practice. In the exchange of ideas in the world of affairs there must be both a giving and a receiving; the two should balance. We should not overlook the fact that the law of compensation is an eternal verity. In the use of Science of Mind one should wish to do only that which is right, and accept nothing less than a constructive program. Having complied with this program one is in a position to expect success and should use the Law for the direct purpose of bringing success into one's experience.

It is wrong to be unsuccessful, but success also means more than dollars and cents. Success means mental growth and spiritual attainment, and includes an abundance of those things which make living enjoyable. As the greater includes the lesser, so mental and spiritual growth includes material success, bringing with it personal happiness and temporal satisfaction.

We cannot avoid the Law so we may as well learn how to use It in the right way. The Law so works that as we believe so we shall experience; if we believe in our abundance we shall receive much, and vice versa. A small concept will provide a small container for the good we wish to receive. Great things are accomplished through great concepts. We wish to succeed and we have a right to be successful. But we can express Reality and partake of Its abundance only as we express freedom, not bondage.

Science of Mind connects Life with living, and spiritual Reality with what we are doing. We must remember that no knowledge is of value unless used. If we *know* a truth we can prove it, for that which we cannot prove we only suppose to be true. To the businessman investigating the possibilities of

Science of Mind there must come a guarantee that its teaching is effective in the affairs of everyday life.

It is a mistake to suppose that some things are material while others are spiritual and that a sharp line can be drawn between matter and Spirit. Matter is Spirit in form; conditions, Spirit in many forms. Spirit expresses Itself in everything; there is no dividing line between form and substance. The best business methods evolved for the handling of affairs are the ones nearest the nature of spiritual Reality— God. One should not be engaged in anything that he feels could contradict that which is good. All legitimate business, constructively handled, is in accord with the highest good.

When we know that our business is an activity of the Spirit working through us we shall be viewing our business in the right light. When we are certain that the things in which we are interested are constructive we should go ahead with complete assurance of success. The only power there is is with us, for there is no power opposed to Spirit.

In a spiritual mind treatment for success we resolve things into ideas, conditions into states of thought, and act upon the premise that the thought is father to the thing. This method is both direct and effective and when rightly used becomes a law unto the thing thought of.

But in doing this we often contact obstacles, negative ideas in our thought which rob us of our good if we retain them. For instance, we sometimes come up against the thought of competition, the belief that there are too many people engaged in the line of business in which we are involved. Competition is a belief that there is not enough good to go around, and while believed in this thought manifests itself as limitation.

We must resolve and dissolve this thought into its native nothingness, for it has no validity in a limitless universe. God does not compete with anyone. Therefore we should not allow the thought to enter our minds that we are competing with anyone. We should never confine ourselves to watching what others are doing or how they are doing it, for when we do this we are limiting our own possibilities to the range of their vision. We must affirmatively guide our activities and not be bound by what anyone else thinks or does. We rob ourselves when we limit our good to the good of someone else, or refuse to admit a greater good than we have ever before experienced.

In spiritual mind treatment we are to think from the viewpoint of a limitless Power, letting It operate through our own minds. Spirit is not bound by anything that has gone before. It is always doing something in a new and better way. We are to let It conceive of new ideas through us and let the Law produce the forms in our experience.

In the business world everything is an exchange of ideas.

The buyer wishes to purchase an idea, the seller has one for sale. Unless this were true nothing could be sold or purchased. Everything begins with an idea. These ideas exist in the One Mind and when one unifies with them they become a part of his experience. We *know* the ones who need our ideas will come to us, or we shall be directed to them. We abide in perfect confidence. Then some thought may come to us which says: Go to a certain person and talk the idea over with him. We must act on this thought, for this is the way the Spirit works. It is working through us and for us.

When an idea to act comes to the mind the act should follow immediately, but without hurry or worry, for confidence is the keynote to success. Business is built upon faith—faith in life, faith in people, and faith in oneself and what one is doing. Without faith there could be no business, no activity, no life—nothing.

If one is engaged in a business in which he has no faith he should get out of it and into something else to which he can give his entire faith and enthusiasm. He should expect success, think success, and talk success, refusing to listen to anything which contradicts success.

The outpush of Mind through human activities is the Self-realization of Spirit and when so understood this outpush becomes *invincible*. Ideas come from the great Mind through the human mind. *The two are really One.* But ideas can come *only to the mentality that expects them* and that opens its doors of thought to them so they can enter and pass through into expression.

Let the mind be open and receptive. Let us court the inner consciousness until its wooing draws from the higher field of realization an inspiration that is *real*. Conviction ever comes from this inner light.

We cannot convince another unless we are first convinced. The person who wishes to sell *must first sell himself to himself and his idea to himself*. His idea is then sold to the world for he is working in a field of unity.

Convince yourself first; the rest follows.

18.

An Answer to
Every Problem

It has been said that the only news we have from heaven
has come through the consciousness of man, and this
saying is true. The march of civilization, the advance of science, the creation of new and better concepts of God, are
emanations of the original Intelligence through the intellect
of man.

Since the dawn of human consciousness progress has
rested in the mind of man. No new creation, no invention,
no art, literature, or science has come from any other source.
From this it would seem as though the mind of man were
the sole agent, and yet, when we note that the same impulses
and emotions are stirring different generations and races
into action, when we perceive that a truth gained by the

mind of one man may be instantly recognized and used by all, we are led to the deeper realization that there is an infinite Mind seeking outlet through all, operating in all and governing all. The reason why it appears as though the mind of man were the sole agent is that the mind of man is the highest form of intelligent outlet we know of for the universal Mind.

What beings there are beyond us in the scale of cosmic evolution we can only guess, but it seems logical to suppose the existence of beings whose consciousness transcends ours as ours trancends that of the tadpole or the mud turtle, but here in the life which we now lead, or in any life which we ever shall lead, the universal Mind proclaims Itself to us through us. Hence any question we shall ever ask, even though it be answered by God Himself, must be answered directly through the mind of man. Each individual gives voice to that which his own consciousness perceives, each has access to the same original Source, each goes as far as he can, and before and within each lies a limitless possibility of further evolvement.

The infinite Mind must contain an answer to every legitimate question. Infinite Intelligence knows and will willingly respond to any and every properly made request. We have immediate access to this Intelligence and in a very real sense the answer to every question is potential within us, because we are within It. We should learn to consciously draw upon It.

The reason no man has yet fully plumbed the depths of his own mind lies in the fact that his mind merges with the Universal and we can never encompass the Infinite. Herein is the possibility of everlasting unfoldment, the glorious concept of an eternal emergence in ever-widening circles. There is no circle so great but that another may be drawn around it. The questions which are unanswered today will be answered tomorrow. More questions will take their place and they in turn will be answered.

In seeking answers to our problems and questions we need to realize and know: There is an Intelligence in me which knows the answer to every question. There is nothing unknown to this Mind. *It has the solution to every problem.* This Mind is my mind. *It is now working in me, through me.* It is acquainting my intellect, my conscious mind, with the desired information.

The riddle of the universe is a paradox. The question is its own answer, for the mind that asks the question is also of the Mind that answers it.

There is a place in the mind which reaches and unifies with the Spirit of pure Intelligence. Spiritual mind treatment is for the purpose of penetrating this inner intuitive perception, thus allowing it to descend into the intellect or conscious mind. The subjective state of our thought, being the result of our accumulated experiences, may or may not be in a state of peace. Hence it becomes necessary for the spiritual mind treatment to penetrate and permeate even the subjective currents of our thought.

When our treatment or prayer stops in the area of mere remembrances we simply rehearse our own accumulated experiences and those of the race mind. Hence our treatment may degenerate into a mild form of daydreaming, perhaps pleasant but generally unproductive. Treatment seeks to penetrate into the realms of the original creative Spirit, to communicate or blend its atmosphere in perfect unity with the original Source of knowledge.

Spiritual mind treatment differs from the average prayer in this: The average prayer *beseeches*, while treatment *acknowledges and accepts*. But effective prayer or treatment in its highest form is the simple and direct communion of man's soul or spirit with the Over-Soul or Spirit. There is no possibility of illusion in true prayer and treatment since it plunges completely through the present content of thought and is receptive only to the universal Mind. That such prayer and meditation find a corresponding response from some indwelling or overdwelling Intelligence is an undeniable experience. The greatest minds of the ages have proved this fact beyond any question of doubt and each one of us may prove it for ourself if we give proper time and attention to the subject.

As love alone knows love, and as that which is beauty in us responds to the beautiful around us, so the mind which sets its vision above the confusion of objective strife meets and unifies with a Presence which knows no strife. It would not be normal to spend one's whole time meditating and praying. The belief in the advisability of doing this is a mistaken idea and arises from one's attempt to separate oneself from the world in which one lives. Meditation should stimulate the intellect to renewed and greater objective action. Thus we should swing from prayer to performance, from meditation into action, from contemplation to accomplishment, until the time comes when thought gradually leads us to a place where we have a continuous sense of an overshadowing Presence and an indwelling Good, forever springing spontaneously into our experience.

If we find ourself surrounded by confusion we should meditate on peace until we feel a sense of peace. Then as the mind returns to its objective state it brings an atmosphere of peace with it which dispels the confusion just as light dispels the darkness. Thus our meditation becomes a practical thing; it has an actual value in everyday experience.

In giving a spiritual mind treatment we meditate upon the essence of pure Spirit and perfect Life until we sense a deep inner calm, until our mind becomes fixed in the real-ization that we are surrounded by perfect Good, by a com-plete and abundant Life, which our mind now contemplates as flowing through us or through the person whom we are seeking to help. Thus we join the atmosphere of our medita-tion with the object of our treatment. We withdraw from the finite and enter the realm of the Infinite, only to return again into the finite with an atmosphere of the Infinite. Thus the relative is expanded and enlightened with the es-sence of pure Being.

At all times we should be certain that in meditation we are not losing the self but that we are merging the lower self with the greater Self, and as time passes we should gradually come to feel that this greater Self is an inseparable compan-ion, an ever-present and ever-available guide on our path-way of human endeavor.

"For God hath not given us the spirit of fear; but of power, and of love, and of a sound mind."

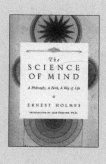
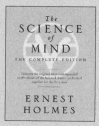

A Treasury of Inspiration and Guidance

A New Design for Living

978-1-58542-814-4

Love and Law

978-1-58542-302-6

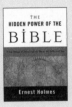

The Hidden Power of the Bible

978-1-58542-511-2

The Essential Ernest Holmes

978-1-58542-181-7

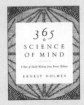

365 Science of Mind

978-1-58542-609-6

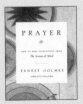

Prayer

978-1-58542-605-8

Simple Guides for Ideas in Action

Creative Mind 978-1-58542-606-5

The Art of Life 978-1-58542-613-3

Creative Mind and Success 978-1-58542-608-9

This Thing Called You 978-1-58542-607-2

Discover a Richer Life 978-1-58542-812-0

Living Without Fear 978-1-58542-813-7

Coming Soon

Questions and Answers on the Science of Mind

Think Your Troubles Away

It's Up to You

Mind Remakes Your World

For more information:
www.penguin.com
www.tarcherbooks.com
www.scienceofmind.com